Eugenia Price's

South

Eugenia Price's
South

A Guide to the People and Places of Her Beloved Region

Mary Bray Wheeler

Foreword by Eugenia Price

Providence House Publishers
PROVIDENCE PUBLISHING CORPORATION
FRANKLIN, TENNESSEE

For my parents,
Frances Dority Bray and Orion James Bray,
who gave me the love I have for
Eugenia Price's South

Originally published by Longstreet Press, Inc., Marietta, Ga. 30067. 1st printing 1993, 2nd printing 1994

Printed in the United States of America

09   08   07   06   05   1   2   3   4   5

Library of Congress Control Number: 2005905472

ISBN: 1-57736-356-6

The author and publisher wish to thank Brion and Beverly Trainor and the BookMark bookstore, St. Simons Island, Georgia, for their support of this project.

The photographs by David King Gleason previously appeared in *Antebellum Homes of Georgia* (Baton Rouge: Louisiana State University Press, 1987). Used by permission of David King Gleason.

Cover design: Joey McNair
Cover photograph: Merriam A. Bass

PROVIDENCE HOUSE PUBLISHERS
an imprint of
Providence Publishing Corporation
238 Seaboard Lane • Franklin, Tennessee 37067
www.providence-publishing.com
800-321-5692

Contents

Illustrations

Photographs

Maps

Figures

Foreword

The minute I learned that my friend Mary Bray Wheeler was going to write this book, I realized how many years I have longed for something more in depth than tour folders and pick-up maps for my readers who travel long distances just to see the places about which I've written in my novels. It has certainly been no secret to me that thousands of people do come from many parts of the United States, Canada—even Europe—in order to discover for themselves what's left of the now distant, far simpler life once lived along the coast of Georgia and Florida. They come, fall in love with the area, then write to me in what I can only call loving detail about their trips.

But often they write before they leave home, asking where to find certain St. Simons Island landmarks, the little church at Frederica, Margaret's chapel near Green Cove Springs in Florida, and so on. And since the four books in the *Savannah Quartet* take place, in part, farther north in Georgia than the coast, these pages include valuable information not only on Savannah, the historic coastal city, but the fertile, lovely land around the site of the old Stiles home near Cartersville, the Cherokees' little reconstructed town of New Echota, the handsome Vann House, and Godfrey Barnsley's legendary gardens where he and his family, including his mother-in-law, Savannah's nineteenth-century social queen, Julia Scarbrough, once lived.

Not only will it be satisfying to me that my loyal readers now have access to Mary Wheeler's carefully and lovingly done book, there is simply no way visitors won't be helped by it. For travel related to any of my historical novels, I will now be able to tell readers that their sightseeing problems are solved, because Mary has written this entire book in response to questions relating to all that still stands to be seen. She has also written it as a reader who, over the years, has become my friend.

More, perhaps far more than its value to those of you who come here, or who may be planning to come, *Eugenia Price's South* will greatly benefit the thousands of devoted friends who read my books, but are, for varying reasons, unable to travel. You who cannot actually visit may now do the very best next thing by reading this book. I have of course, read every line with joy and delight, not only because my work caught the attention of a writer of Mary Bray Wheeler's caliber, but because I can tell you that what she has written is accurate and clear. It has also captured the spirit of what I try to give to you, year after year, on page after page as I sit working at this desk. Mary's book is far more than a travel guide or companion. Because of her writing skills and her own love of the area, you who cannot make the journey in person will be enabled to make it in your imaginations.

I and my own research assistant, Nancy Goshorn, have tried to stay in close touch with Mary throughout her vast amount of work; and if I lack authority on most things, I am the authority on these novels of mine and can assure you that she has exceeded my expectations. Mary has read and reread my novels, she has gone herself to every locale, she has talked at length with those who gave me of their expertise in all my own research throughout the years, and now, thanks to my friends at Longstreet Press, the splendid results of her work are ready for you to absorb and enjoy.

Doubleday has recently published an extra, nonfiction book of mine titled *Inside One Author's Heart*. I wrote it from my heart to you, the thousands of faithful readers with whom I share an almost mystical bond. Certainly our bond is strong, and most in the publishing world tell me it is unique. Mary Wheeler has actually met many of you at various events, because her interest in my work has brought her to book signings and parties in numerous cities where you and I have come to know each other. Mary has stood for hours, just watching us grow acquainted, has heard you as a reader declare your loyalty to me as an author you happen to like. She understands our special bond. See for yourself in these pages that she understands *us* as we really are. She also cares.

Eugenia Price
St. Simons Island, Georgia
February 1993

About the Eugenia Price/Joyce K. Blackburn Charitable Foundation

The Eugenia Price/Joyce K. Blackburn Charitable Foundation, Inc., was established to ensure the perpetuation of the accomplishments and the commitments of the founders. The Foundation's primary work is to continue the literary legacy that has enriched the lives of millions of people. The work of these two authors includes fifty-seven titles that have been published in eighteen languages and printed in excess of fifty million copies worldwide. The Foundation intends to make available in print these Christian inspirational, historical fiction, juvenile, and biographical works so that new generations of readers may be enriched by the authors' combined works.

Proceeds from the Foundation are used to fund grants, scholarships, and contributions to charitable groups. All Foundation programs, events, and activities perpetuate, promote, and support the memory and achievements of these two beloved writers. The Foundation accepts tax-exempt donations which will fund its work. Contributions may be made to:

Eugenia Price/Joyce K. Blackburn Charitable Foundation, Inc.
c/o Eileen Humphlett, Executive Director
400 Stevens Road
St. Simons Island, Georgia 31522

Map 1. Eugenia Price's South

Discovering Eugenia Price's South

P eople have always loved to travel. As long as there have been lives to live, there have been explorers; as long as there have been stories to tell, there have been listeners; as long as there have been books to write, there have been readers. And as long as there have been novels by Eugenia Price, there have been growing numbers of people, all over the world, who have journeyed across time and space—page by page, book by book, mile by mile—into Eugenia Price's South.

I know how it began for me, in the 1970s, as a new "convert" to Eugenia Price's novels. A group of friends and I were eager to locate some of the memorable settings with which Price had won our hearts. By early spring of 1977 we had completed our plans. Approaching our upcoming trip with the madness of college students cramming for final exams, we studied background material so we could be as informed as possible. Our starting place was *James Edward Oglethorpe*, a biography of the Georgia founder written in 1970 by Joyce Blackburn. The afterword to *Lighthouse* mentioned her book, and reading it made me aware of how important St. Simons Island and Fort Frederica were in protecting colonial Georgia, indeed all the colonies, from Spanish invasion. That enlightening volume was the perfect introductory material, for by then we were more serious than ever about the island's history.

Anticipation heightened as we reserved a St. Simons Island kitchenette apartment for a week. At long last it was time to head for Georgia. Once there, we settled in and immediately put our master plan into action. Armed with two complete sets of the *St. Simons Trilogy*, a copy of *Oglethorpe*, a roll of rice paper, a block of graphite, and a can of spray-on fixative, we headed for Christ Church cemetery. No matter what else we accomplished, we wanted to do tombstone rubbings that we could frame and use to prove to any doubters back in Tennessee that we really had made this journey. We did forget one thing, however—the insect repellent. Those island gnats weren't a bit happy that we were crawling and squatting among the ivy-choked paths where the Goulds were "resting in peace." We went back at dawn (swollen ankles, hands, and all) to finish our keepsakes. Before breakfast we had permanently affixed at least one gnat to each of the finished graphite rubbings: the gravestone of James Gould, the lighthouse builder, and the marker with a chiseled rose that Horace Bunch Gould had had carved for his sister Mary. I simply had to have a reminder of Mary's strength for my den wall.

(Of course, for years my younger son thought this piece of art facing his highchair was from a family member's grave. When his kindergarten teacher asked if anyone could read, Shannon raised his hand and announced, "I can read Aunt Mary's tombstone on the wall at home. It says, 'TO MY SISTER MARY E. H. GOULD.'" I was called to the school for a conference.)

For an entire week we soaked up literally any and all details about that beloved, light-filled island setting. Naturally, like most of her readers, we hoped beyond hope that maybe, just maybe, the best of all possible luck would be ours and we would actually get to see Eugenia Price. The closest we came was during that early morning trek to finish our tombstone rubbings at the cemetery. Right in the path, as we were leaving, was a gorgeous non-pareil, exactly like those in the trilogy, and we were convinced this was the very same multicolored, painted bunting from Eugenia Price's yard, the one she called "Richard." We were ecstatic.

What is the mystique that surrounds Eugenia Price and her readers? Folk just like me journey across America and from around the globe to St. Simons Island, Georgia, to see the lighthouse and keeper's cottage, the ruins of the slave hospital at Retreat Plantation, and the Couper, Dodge, Gould, and other chiseled gravemarkers in the cemetery at Christ Church, Frederica. Visitors flock to St. Augustine and Jacksonville in north Florida tracking any evidence of Maria, Don Juan McQueen, or Margaret Seton Fleming. In Savannah readers search for Harris, Mackay, McQueen, and Browning graves among the monuments at Colonial Park and Laurel Grove cemeteries, take nostalgic strolls along Factor's Walk, and absorb the beauty of the mansions and churches along Oglethorpe's carefully laid-out squares. In north Georgia, Cassville, Cartersville, Adairsville, and New Echota attract those who want to see where the Latimer family lived and what enticed Savannah's elite (among them the Stiles and Barnsley families) to relocate in the former Cherokee nation. What mysterious fascination causes readers to search for a lonely Civil War gravesite in Roswell; the towering rice-mill chimney at Butler Island past Darien on the Altamaha River; the mansion ruins at Cumberland Island, reached only by ferry; or, just north of Jacksonville on Fort Georgia Island, the home of Don Juan McQueen?

Eugenia Price readers know that two themes dominate her novels: First is the sense of home and belonging that the main characters seek to establish for themselves and their families; second is the growth and development of a sense of faith and providence at work in their lives. These themes of home and faith are so compelling because the author identifies personally with her characters. Eugenia Price writes from her own understanding about the universal need for faith and longing for homecoming not only in a modern, fast-paced world but throughout human history. The twelve novels in *Eugenia Price's South* span America's beginning years as a nation. They are woven threads of belonging, of faith, and of establishing a sense of home. Relationships with people and pla transcend separations of distance and even death.

This guidebook is designed as a companion for readers journeying through Eugenia Price's South. One purpose is to introduce you, the reader/traveler, to the vast arena from which the characters are drawn and to give you a glimpse into the emergence of their plantations, homes, businesses, churches, and towns. Written particularly for the many readers who travel to the sites where Price sets her masterful stories, this guide will provide both historical information and precise travel directions to the sites that you are so eager to experience firsthand.

Many readers have been just as curious to know more about the real people behind Price's characters, and this guide provides a biographical sketch of these fascinating historical figures. As the chapters discuss each trilogy or quartet of novels, historical and fictional characters are distinguished, but together, the whole cast of Eugenia Price's characters creates a credible portrayal of eighteenth- and nineteenth-century life in the South. Price created her fictional families and individuals so realistically that their biographies are not easy to distinguish from the true ones, as you will see in the narrative portions of this guidebook.

An array of illustrative material—maps, charts, photographs, timelines, and a complete cast of characters—accompanies the text. The maps not only provide a general orientation to Price's Southern settings but pinpoint exact locations to guide readers to the various sites they will want to visit. Finally, with so many people and places reappearing in different novels and groups of novels, the index will be especially helpful to ensure that you find all the available information on a particular character or site.

The text of this book is organized by trilogy or quartet. Part 1 covers five novels about St. Simons Island, Georgia, probably the best loved of all destinations for Eugenia Price readers. A barrier island between the south Georgia mainland and the Atlantic Ocean, St. Simons Island is the primary setting for the *St. Simons Trilogy* (*Lighthouse, New Moon Rising,* and *The Beloved Invader*) and the first two novels in the planned *Georgia Trilogy* (*Bright Captivity* and *Where Shadows Go*).

Part 2 is set in northeast Florida and covers the *Florida Trilogy* (*Maria*, *Don Juan McQueen*, and *Margaret's Story*). These novels are an interesting example of how Price's characters weave in and out of her stories, creating a sturdy colorful tapestry. The latter pages of *Maria* introduce you to a winsome figure named John McQueen, whose life in Florida is central to *Don Juan McQueen*, Price's novel that bears his Spanish name. How fascinating to remember him from *Lighthouse* when, during a rare visit to St. Simons Island, McQueen meets and hires young James Gould to manage the Los Molinos saw mills, McQueen's holding on the St. Mary's River at the Georgia/Florida border.

Part 3 is based in Savannah. The *Savannah Quartet* also covers the development of north Georgia areas by characters (both factual and fictionalized) from Savannah and coastal Georgia. Readers are always delighted to discover that Don Juan's daughter, Eliza McQueen Mackay, is the matriarch of the *Savannah Quartet* (*Savannah*, *To See Your Face Again*, *Before Darkness Falls*, and *Stranger in Savannah*). When Eliza's children speak of their heritage, readers, too, recall enjoying the colorful life of their Grandfather McQueen in the novels about Spanish East Florida. If the first Price novels you read were the *Savannah Quartet*, your interest in meeting the charming Don Juan will lead you straight to the earlier novels.

Traditionally, people in the South don't say good-bye, they say, "Why don't you come on and go home with us?" When Eugenia Price discovered a place so intriguing that she moved there from Chicago, she must have known that all those "permanent residents" of St. Simons and St. Augustine and Savannah were saying to her, "Come on home." She bonded with her characters by building her home among them to live out her days writing their stories. She has brought to life generations of faith-filled, strong people in the very locale where they lived out their days. Remember that whether you are traveling by armchair or in person, now or anytime in the future, Eugenia Price's people and places are just waiting for you to come by for a visit.

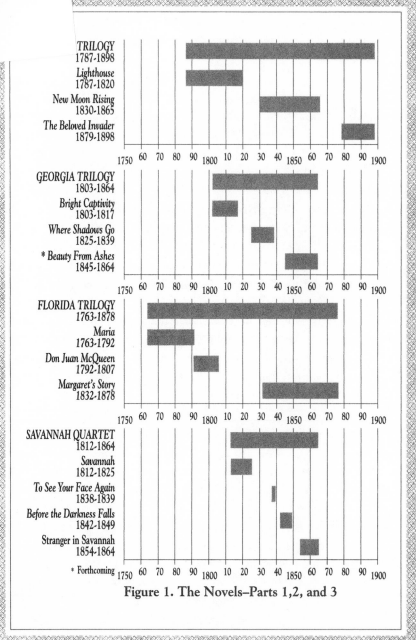

TRILOGY
1787-1898

Lighthouse
1787-1820

New Moon Rising
1830-1865

The Beloved Invader
1879-1898

1750 60 70 80 90 1800 10 20 30 40 1850 60 70 80 90 1900

GEORGIA TRILOGY
1803-1864

Bright Captivity
1803-1817

Where Shadows Go
1825-1839

* *Beauty From Ashes*
1845-1864

1750 60 70 80 90 1800 10 20 30 40 1850 60 70 80 90 1900

FLORIDA TRILOGY
1763-1878

Maria
1763-1792

Don Juan McQueen
1792-1807

Margaret's Story
1832-1878

1750 60 70 80 90 1800 10 20 30 40 1850 60 70 80 90 1900

SAVANNAH QUARTET
1812-1864

Savannah
1812-1825

To See Your Face Again
1838-1839

Before the Darkness Falls
1842-1849

Stranger in Savannah
1854-1864

* Forthcoming 1750 60 70 80 90 1800 10 20 30 40 1850 60 70 80 90 1900

Figure 1. The Novels–Parts 1,2, and 3

Eugenia Price's
South

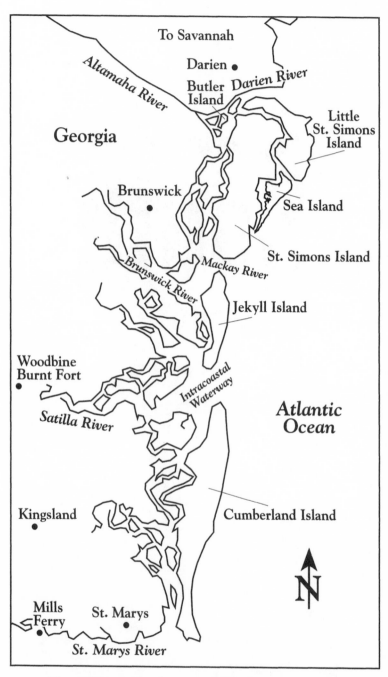

To Savannah

Darien

Altamaha River

Butler Island

Darien River

Little St. Simons Island

Georgia

Brunswick

Sea Island

St. Simons Island

Mackay River

Brunswick River

Jekyll Island

Woodbine
Burnt Fort

Intracoastal Waterway

Atlantic Ocean

Satilla River

Kingsland

Cumberland Island

N

Mills Ferry

St. Marys

St. Marys River

Map 2. Part 1–St. Simons Trilogy/Georgia Trilogy

P~ART~ 1

St. Simons Trilogy
Georgia Trilogy

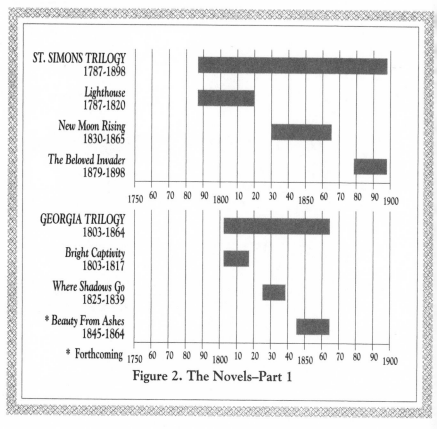

Figure 2. The Novels–Part 1

CHAPTER 1

The Novels

LIGHTHOUSE
NEW MOON RISING
THE BELOVED INVADER
BRIGHT CAPTIVITY
WHERE SHADOWS GO
BEAUTY FROM ASHES

O ur visit to Eugenia Price's South begins where she began in her novels—St. Simons Island, Georgia. As most readers already know, Price started the *St. Simons Trilogy* with *The Beloved Invader*, a true story from the Reconstruction years that followed the Civil War. Her next two books, *New Moon Rising* then *Lighthouse*, worked back in time to the early plantation era. Seven novels later she returned to the planters and plantations of St. Simons Island. In her planned *Georgia Trilogy*—*Bright Captivity*, *Where Shadows Go*, and *Beauty From Ashes*—parallel accounts from that same post-colonial period further elucidate the intertwining St. Simons Island saga that began captivating readers more than twenty-five years ago.

Our trip to St. Simons Island follows James Gould, a young man from post-Revolution Granville, Massachusetts. In 1787 Gould, who could only imagine the beauty and warmth of lands to the south, also dreamed of building bridges and lighthouses from his own designs and plans. In *Lighthouse*, a series of events and some valuable new connections took him south to St. Simons Island; he was head of a crew hired to identify and procure live oak timber for the first U.S. naval vessels. Gould's ultimate goal was to bring to reality his own design for an octagonal lighthouse.

Gould developed a special bond with a wealthy St. Simons planter, hospitable John Couper of Cannon's Point Plantation, which would be crucial to his dream of building a lighthouse. Couper had come to the island from Scotland, by way of Savannah, in the early 1790s and identified with Gould's enthusiasm for establishing a home and making a name for himself. James Gould lived at Cannon's Point for a time with Couper and his family. Their loyal friendship proved a valuable asset to each of these men, their families, and the life of the island.

Lighthouse follows Gould's decision to settle on St. Simons Island and the establishment of the plantation home he called New St. Clair. Eugenia Price delineates for the reader Gould's determination and stamina, his sources of stability, and the eventual accomplishment of his goal—the building of the lighthouse he had designed as a young boy. As he matures, Gould becomes increasingly committed to his home, family, and deepening faith.

New Moon Rising follows the struggle of James Gould's son Horace to find his own place in life. Horace discovered that for him, as for his father, security revolved around home and family and Christ Church, Frederica. New St. Clair and the adjoining Gould plantation, Black Banks, emerge as worthy forces in Horace's decision to claim St. Simons Island as his own place to be. This novel carries the island families through the tragic Civil War years, their evacuation from the island, and the inherent destruction and loss so identified with that era. Somehow Horace Gould managed to bring his family home to St. Simons after the war and to begin rebuilding their lives.

Reconstruction sets the scene for *The Beloved Invader*. Some fourteen years after Horace Gould returned from battle to find the island and its beautiful church all but totally destroyed, an outsider entered the story. Anson Dodge visited St. Simons to inspect his father's prosperous Dodge-Meigs Lumber Mills operation at the former Hamilton Plantation site on Gascoigne Bluff. Becoming intrigued with the island and its people, Dodge decided to make a home there for himself and his soon-to-be bride. This novel builds on Dodge's relationship with Horace Gould and the parishioners of Christ Church, Frederica, on St. Simons. Dodge and his fiancé planned to return to their island home following a wedding trip to India. After the tragic death of his bride, Dodge vowed to rebuild Christ Church to honor her memory. This "beloved invader" became the rector of Christ Church and eventually married Horace Gould's daughter.

The Beloved Invader introduces us to a rather bitter couple, Emma and P. D. Bass. Two of Eugenia Price's few fictional characters, the Basses were necessary to a plot set during the years following the Civil War on St. Simons Island. After Dodge had his first encounter with them, Horace Bunch Gould commented, "They're part of our Island. I've always felt I needed P.D. and his wife to keep me cut down to size."

Bright Captivity, the first in the *Georgia Trilogy,* returns to the early 1800s and Cannon's Point. Following the British occupation of St. Simons at the close of the War of 1812, John Couper's daughter Anne married another "invader," British marine lieutenant John Fraser. First living in England, the Frasers eventually emigrated to St. Simons Island. Despite John Fraser's nostalgic longing to return to military life, his love for Anne and her sense of home compelled him to accept John Couper's island plantation way of life for himself and his family.

Where Shadows Go covers the heart of the island's plantation days continuing the Couper/Fraser family saga. Price's forthcoming book, *Beauty From Ashes,* the final book in the *Georgia Trilogy,* will take these families through the Civil War period.

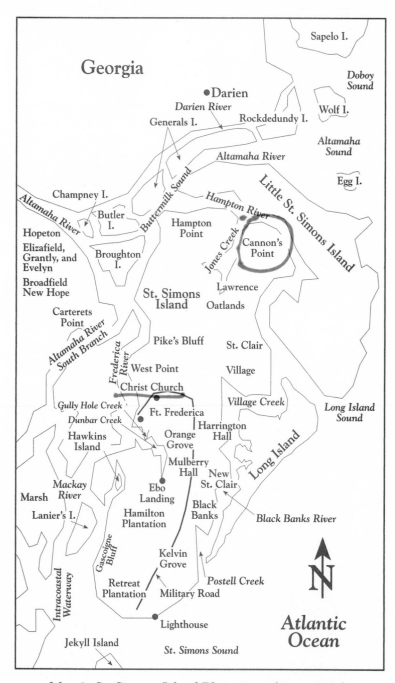

Map 3. St. Simons Island Plantations (circa 1860)

CHAPTER 2

People and Places

St. Simons Island, Georgia

Early Days

Menendez de Aviles, governor of Florida, sent Spanish friars from the order of St. Francis to build a mission on St. Simons Island as early as 1566. These newcomers called the island's native inhabitants Guale (pronounced *Wallie*) Indians. The Native Americans knew the island as Asao, but the Spaniards called it San Simons, or St. Simons.

For more than a hundred years the brown-robed monks lived and worked among the Indians. Unrest and tension plagued the settlement, mainly due to an influx of raiders from the British Isles and the West Indies on their way to the Carolina colony farther up the coast. Indians and priests alike finally deserted St. Simons.

Frederica

In 1733 British general James Edward Oglethorpe established the colony of Georgia. He brought settlers to St. Simons where together they built the town and fort that Oglethorpe designed and named Frederica. The Indians and Spaniards had developed a building material from common substances at hand—sand, water, and oyster shells—and Oglethorpe adapted this cement-like mixture, called tabby, for his own construction uses. Tabby proved to make strong foundations and walls for homes and businesses at Frederica.

Spanish Franciscan missionaries once had preached to Guale Indians under giant moss-draped live oak trees; now Church of England ministers Charles and John Wesley conducted services for English colonists and members of Oglethorpe's regiment at Frederica. This was the origin of Christ Church, Frederica.

Indians who inhabited the nearby coastal islands received Oglethorpe openly. His alliance with them contributed to the successful defense of St. Simons against threatened Spanish invasion. Oglethorpe's British Regulars combined its forces with the Indians to win a significant victory over the Spanish in the Battle of Bloody Marsh (c. 1742). Scottish Highland Rangers from the nearby mainland settlement of Darien also contributed to the British win. The fighting took place along the Military Road from Fort St. Simons on the south end of the island as far north as Gully Hole Creek near Fort Frederica. Here, in a surprise attack, Oglethorpe's men drove the Spanish south in a disorderly retreat to a spot now called Bloody Marsh, where they were soundly defeated.

In 1749 the Frederica Regiment was disbanded and began to withdraw; the town of Frederica then started to fade. Now that the land was considered safe from attack, new settlers were drawn to the area and received land grants on the mainland and the remainder of St. Simons Island.

Following the Revolution, investors and planters purchased many of the original land grants in vast tracts, bringing about the great plantation era along the Southern coast of the young nation. The colonial planters were encouraged by the lush vegetation native to the area. More important to them was the survival of fruit trees and other plants that long-ago Spanish friars had brought to experiment with in the fertile soil of the New World.

Frewin-Stevens Property

Frederica was virtually deserted by 1820 when two former British citizens, Capt. James Frewin and his wife, Sarah Dorothy Hay, started purchasing parcels of land at "Old Town." By 1824 Captain Frewin had a house, a tavern, and a store at the old Frederica wharf. In 1828 he bought all the lots designated as Old Fort, after which he gradually bought adjoining lots in Frederica from original grant holders. An important addition to this family was an orphaned niece and namesake of Sarah Frewin, Sarah Dorothy Hay, who came to live with her aunt in 1838. Young Sarah later married Capt. Charles Stevens. Stevens, whose schooners carried shipments for the planters along the coast between Savannah and St. Marys, also became a landowner and planter. Eventually the Frewin-Stevens family owned all of the original Frederica.

Sarah Frewin died in England in 1854. Capt. James Frewin refused to leave the island during the Civil War, became ill, was discovered just prior to his death by a Federal ship's surgeon, and was

View of ruins at Fort Frederica National Monument, St. Simons Island. (Courtesy of Genon Hickerson Neblett)

buried at Christ Churchyard in 1863. Captain Stevens refused to pilot Federal patrol boats, was taken prisoner, and died at Fort Delaware in 1865. Sarah Stevens was postmistress at Frederica after the war, and at her death all the Frewin–Stevens property was inherited and divided by children of the Stevens family.

The Frederica portion went to a daughter, Belle Stevens Taylor, who in 1903 gave the ruins of Old Fort to the Georgia Society of Colonial Dames of America. Organized in 1941, the Fort Frederica Association raised funds to purchase the land around the fort. These two groups presented the fort and grounds to the National Parks Service, and, in 1947, the site became Fort Frederica National Monument. In 1954 the Fort Frederica Association acquired and added the Battle of Bloody Marsh site to the National Parks System.

Christ Church, Frederica

This congregation began in 1736 as a mission of the Church of England. Rev. Charles Wesley conducted the first services in a chapel at Fort Frederica. His brother, Rev. John Wesley, was the rector at Christ Church, Savannah, and also served Frederica.

After the Revolution this church and others formed the Protestant Episcopal Church in the United States of America. Christ Church organized in 1807 and was incorporated by the Georgia State Legislature on December 22, 1808.

Wardens of the new church were Dr. Robert Grant of Oatlands Plantation and Maj. William Page of Retreat. Those serving on the first vestry were George Abbott of Frederica; John Couper of Cannon's Point; Raymond Demere, Jr., of Mulberry Grove; James Hamilton of Hamilton Plantation; and Joseph Turner, collector of the ports of Frederica and Brunswick. A list of subscribers to the church included other planters and citizens.

Rev. Dr. William Best was the first rector of Christ Church, Frederica. Best served the parish in those years before the War of 1812 when embargoes caused severe problems for coastal planters. Before a church could be built, the church's organizers held services at subscriber John Beck's house on the location of Orange Hall, the only dwelling General Oglethorpe had owned in Georgia. The church paid Beck $1.50 a week for the use of his home and the necessary preparation for services.

Rev. Edmund Matthews followed Rev. Dr. Best in 1810 as the next rector. Matthews was one of three clergy who organized the diocese of Georgia in 1823. During his stay, a small white church with green shutters and a belfry were built; not only did it serve as a house of worship but also became the center of life for the island. The weekly gathering began as early as nine o'clock on Sunday mornings. The women caught up on island news, the children played, and the men gathered under the giant, live oak trees to read the mail and to discuss current happenings gleaned from the postmaster at Frederica, George Abbott.

At age twenty-four, Rev. Theodore B. Bartow, who had taken his ordination vows in South Carolina, became rector of Christ Church, Frederica. Arriving on St. Simons Island in July 1830, he replaced Rev. Mr. Motte and was well loved and respected. Bartow married Isabella Hamilton Couper (1815–41). Belle, as she was called by her family and close friends, was the daughter of Rebecca and John Couper of Cannon's Point.

Built in 1820, the first church on the present site was almost completely destroyed during the Civil War. Following the war, evening prayers were read each Sunday in the home of Horace Bunch Gould of Black Banks Plantation. Gould had been one of the first to return to the island after the war.

The Rev. Anson Green Phelps Dodge, Jr., was responsible for the restoration and building now in use. Part of the Credence Table and an inset in the present altar were salvaged from the ruins of the 1820 building. Erected in 1884 as a memorial to Dodge's wife Ellen, the new church has a cruciform design with a trussed gothic roof.

The beautiful new church was consecrated in 1886 by the Right Reverend J. W. Beckwith, Episcopal bishop of Georgia. Beckwith greatly respected Anson Dodge for his generosity of money and time in establishing more than thirty such missions across Georgia. In the churchyard cemetery, markers bear the names of the island families and the rectors of Christ Church so identified with St. Simons history.

Against this diverse background of Indians, Spanish monks,

Rev. Anson G. P. Dodge, beloved rector of Christ Church, Frederica. (Courtesy of the Coastal Georgia Historical Society)

Ellen A. P. Dodge, first wife of Rev. Anson Dodge. (Courtesy of the Coastal Georgia Historical Society)

General Oglethorpe, Frederica, cotton plantations, and Christ Church, Eugenia Price has brought to life the people who made St. Simons their home. Her characters are many and colorful: the few remaining citizens of Frederica (by then called Old Town and Old Fort); plantation owners, merchants, craftsmen, and clergy from countries far away and from the colonies to the north; slaves, indentured servants, and laborers imported as property by traders seeking fortunes in their own ways; and finally the ensuing families who grew and developed and survived through this author's imagination and honest portrayal.

The Plantation Era

Because the plantation culture was the dominant way of life for coastal Georgians in the eighteenth and nineteenth centuries, the characters in the *St. Simons* and *Georgia* trilogies are presented according to the plantation on which they lived. Relying on early records of land grants and deeds, I have organized the plantations by the time period in which they were established, rather than list them alphabetically or rank them in order of importance. A chronology of plantation ownership (Figure 3) is included to show the order we will follow, and Map 3 is a visual display of the plantations along the Altamaha River and on St. Simons Island circa 1860. (The quickest way to find a particular person or place would be to use the index.)

Just prior to the nineteenth century, large tracts of land were highly accessible to new farmers, and the agricultural needs of the young nation were great. These, among other factors, contributed to the development of the southland's plantations. Because *Lighthouse* is our introduction to plantation life, we will follow James Gould as he arrived in St. Simons and began to learn for himself about the planters, their backgrounds, and the land they owned.

James Gould was the son of James and Kate Gould of Granville, Massachusetts. James' older brother William was killed during the Revolutionary War, and their father eventually died from wounds he had received at Bemis Heights while serving as a captain in the Continental Army. James persuaded his widowed mother to move to Bangor, Massachusetts (later Maine), so James could work and study civil engineering. Before James Gould left Bangor, he built his mother and siblings a good house, and although he was close to his sister Mary, James was determined to find a new life for himself. For years he had longed to travel south; now he needed to leave behind the pain of losing the hand of a bright, lovely Scottish girl named Jessie who had chosen to marry James' younger brother Horace.

James sought out Capt. John Barry, an American naval officer, whose rank at the close of the Revolutionary War was second only to John Paul Jones. Barry's home, Strawberry Hill, was four miles north of Philadelphia, and it was there that James Gould agreed to accompany Captain Barry to Georgia to secure timber for building ships for the first U.S. naval force.

Gould arrived on St. Simons Island in October 1794. Although Oglethorpe's town of Frederica had been the Glynn County seat since

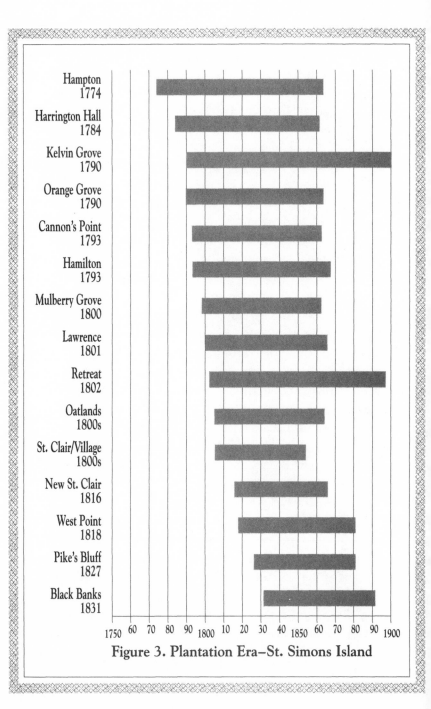

Figure 3. Plantation Era–St. Simons Island

the end of the Revolutionary War, the fort and barracks were in ruins and had been in need of repair since before the last regiment departed in 1767. Gould's job was to survey the island for all available sources of the valuable live oak timber needed for shipbuilding. Live oak had been chosen because it was five times more resilient than the white oak that grew in the northeastern part of the new country.

Gould's first objective was to supervise timber cutting on the southwest side of St. Simons Island. The Gascoigne Bluff sawmill was located on acreage that originally belonged to and was named for Capt. William Gascoigne, the Frederica officer who had been in charge of the ship *Hawk*. Richard Leake owned Gascoigne Bluff and nearby Hawkins Island, granted first to Dr. Thomas Hawkins, Frederica's surgeon. Leake, an absentee owner after he built his house on the mainland, used his St. Simons property as an investment by selling timber rights.

James Gould very quickly ascertained that he would need permission to harvest timber freely from the island in order to fulfill the entire contractual arrangement for shipbuilding. He would also need the help of additional slave labor from the nearby plantations.

John Couper of Cannon's Point befriended the young Gould and helped him learn about each of the St. Simons Island planters. It was John Couper's encouragement that eventually influenced James Gould to settle on St. Simons. Their relationship develops fully throughout Eugenia Price's novels, influencing them, their families, and other islanders through many years.

Although James Gould had come to St. Simons for its live oak timber, he soon learned that the end of the Revolutionary War had initiated a time of agricultural innovation followed by great prosperity. Revenue from crops of long-staple cotton had allowed planters a comfortable, gracious way of life.

Cultivation of this vital crop had begun at Maj. Pierce Butler's Hampton Plantation as early as 1791. Soon other planters, in particular James Spalding, John Couper, and James Hamilton, followed Maj. Butler's lead, and the exceptionally fine quality cotton became known as sea-island cotton. St. Simons cotton was shipped to Liverpool, England, by way of Savannah, Georgia, or Charleston, South

Carolina, and was greatly admired. The Butler cotton was reputed to be of superior grade and consistently produced high revenues.

Hampton Plantation (1774) and Butler Island Plantation (Altamaha River)

Pierce Butler was born in Ireland in 1744, entered the British army in 1761, and by 1766 was a major in His Majesty's Twenty-ninth Regiment stationed in Boston. He resigned the military and settled in Charles Town, South Carolina, prior to the Revolution. There he met and married Mary (Polly) Middleton, daughter of Col. Thomas Middleton.

Major Butler represented South Carolina in the House and the Senate, signed the Constitution of the United States, and was a close associate of George Washington. His holdings in Georgia were Hampton Point (St. Simons Island), Little St. Simons Island, Butler Island (on the Altamaha River near Darien), and Woodville (further up the Altamaha).

Butler Point, 1,700 acres at the northern tip of St. Simons Island, was the location of Major Butler's Hampton Plantation property (known earlier as Hampton Point). This land, first granted to Henry Ellis in 1758, was next deeded to Philip and Jane Delegal; Major Butler bought it in 1774 for 6,000 pounds from the third owners, John and Frances Graham of Savannah, Georgia.

Butler River, also named for Major Butler, was the waterway from the Darien River to the South Altamaha River past Butler Island and on to St. Simons. The Altamaha River makes its way 137 miles from middle Georgia to the Port of Darien. Loggers transported lumber down the waterway, and on its banks were the earliest rice-growing plantations. Butler Island, Butler's 1,500-acre island, was the leading rice plantation in the region south of the Altamaha River below Darien. Although Butler first purchased land in this area in 1774, he did not pursue cultivation until the end of the Revolutionary War.

James Gould stayed for a short time at Hampton Plantation. He soon learned that Butler designed his holdings to be regimental, secure communities that could operate alone. Slaves excelled in all the crafts necessary to supply the plantation with sufficient tools, equipment, clothing, and food to survive independently. The Butler slaves were never allowed to intermingle with servants from other plantations, and their attitude was one of superiority through many generations. Overseers Roswell King, Sr., and his son Roswell King, Jr., though astute in their recordkeeping and business management, had infamous reputations of abject cruelty and harshness to the slaves working the Butler plantations.

The mansion at Hampton was built of tabby and wood and was located on the Hampton River at Jones Creek. Major Butler relished entertaining so much that many guests enjoyed the plantation at his invitation whether or not he could be present.

In 1804, following his duel with Alexander Hamilton, Aaron Burr visited for a month at Hampton Plantation on St. Simons. Pierce Butler and Aaron Burr had long been friends since their days together serving in the U.S. Senate. Burr was vice-president in 1801 under President Thomas Jefferson. Writing to his daughter Theodosia of the luxury at Hampton, Burr particularly commented on the abundance of fruit, fine wines, and sumptuous menus prepared from readily available foods of great variety and quality.

Major Butler's daughter Sally married Dr. James Mease of Philadelphia. They had three sons: Pierce Butler (called Butler), John, and Thomas Mease. Of the major's grandsons, Thomas died in childhood; Butler and John adopted the Butler surname (becoming Pierce Butler II and John Butler), so they could accept their inheritance. Major Butler lost contact with his own son Thomas, and his daughter Frances never married.

The Georgia properties were managed by Roswell King, Sr., and his son Roswell, Jr., so that at the major's death in 1822 the elder Roswell King was co-conservator of the estate with Frances Butler. It was not until her death that the grandsons began annual inspections of their holdings in Georgia. Maj. Pierce Butler is buried in Philadelphia in the churchyard of Christ Church.

After Butler Mease changed his name to Pierce Butler (c. 1826) and claimed his inheritance from his grandfather's estate, he married the famous British actress Fanny Kemble (1834). Francis Henry Fitzhardinge Berkely was the musician who introduced his Philadelphia friend Pierce Butler to Charles Kemble and Kemble's daughter Fanny (c. 1833).

Frances Anne (Fanny) Kemble was the daughter of Charles Kemble (1775–1854), a renowned Shakespearean actor, and his wife, Marie-Therèse de Camp (1774–1838). His sister, Fanny's aunt, was known the world over as the theater's "immortal" Sarah Siddons (1755–1831). Fanny made her debut at Covent Gardens and instantly became London society's number one attraction.

Fanny Kemble met Pierce Butler on tour in America, and a short while later they were married. She seemed to have everything: wealth, talent, beauty, youth, popularity, and a handsome American husband. From December 1838 until April 1839 Fanny Butler spent fifteen weeks in Georgia with her husband and two small daughters, Sally and Fanny. It wasn't long before she began to keep an extensive diary.

The plantations, the near tropical setting, the slaves and their harsh treatment by the overseers—all this commanded her attention and fascination. She was both intrigued and horrified at the same time. Her total opposition to slavery and the conditions she witnessed added fuel to the fires of discontent in the Butler marriage. A rather nasty divorce ended by default on November 21, 1849.

Fanny Kemble Butler's *Journal of a Residence on a Georgian Plantation* was published in 1863, and many believed it to have been the cause of negative opinions about the South in England and America. Much of her thinking was shaped by the Rev. William Ellery Channing (1780–1842). Outspoken in his views against chattel slavery, Channing was minister of the Federal Street Congregational Church in Boston from 1803 until his death in 1842. One of the most forceful pulpit orators and pamphleteers of the nineteenth century, Channing's ideas started the American Unitarian Association. Fanny Kemble Butler returned to England in the mid-1850s and never visited Georgia again.

In 1866, following the Civil War, Pierce Butler and his daughter Frances returned to their Georgia properties and worked to restore them to profitability. Like her mother, Frances Butler wrote of her

18

experiences in nineteenth-century coastal Georgia, and her accounts of Reconstruction days reveal an unusual perception. Her father died in 1867, leaving Frances to manage alone for four years until her marriage to Rev. James Leigh of England in 1871.

Today the Butler Island property is part of the Altamaha Wildfowl Area, which belongs to the State of Georgia. Major Butler's 1,700-acre plantation on St. Simons, purchased more than two hundred years ago, now has been developed in part as a residential area.

Harrington Plantation/Harrington Hall (1784) and Mulberry Grove Plantation (1800)

A 150-acre property that bore the name Harrington belonged to Capt. Raymond Demere of Frederica. The captain named the St. Simons holdings for a friend, Lord Harrington, with whom he had served in Spain. In fact, Captain Demere first honored his friend when he received a prior grant of fifty acres; there he named his home Harrington Hall. After the Revolutionary War the captain's son, Raymond Demere, Jr., developed a third property, Mulberry Grove, on the south end of the island.

Captain Demere and his brother Paul, also a captain, were born in France. Educated in England, they were officers in the Independent Company stationed at Frederica that fought with Oglethorpe at the Battle of Bloody Marsh. Both men were remarkable military heroes, civil servants, and successful planters. Raymond was the first commander of Fort Loudon on the Tennessee River, and he was succeeded in 1757 by Paul. Later, while Raymond was in charge of Fort Frederica, Paul was killed in an ambush on Fort Loudon by Cherokee Indians in 1760.

Raymond and Paul Demere each had a son named Raymond who served in the Revolution. The grandsons of Raymond Demere, Jr. (d. 1829), inherited the Harrington land, and one of the young men, Paul, married Annie Fraser, granddaughter of John Couper of Cannon's Point. Their son John Fraser Demere (b. 1841), a fifth-generation Demere, was born at Harrington Hall.

Unfortunately, nothing remains of the Demere homes, as no

family returned to the island following the Civil War. Harrington Plantation is now a residential section; the site of Harrington Hall bears a marker placed by the Georgia Historical Commission; and part of the old Mulberry Grove land is used by the island's airport.

Kelvin Grove Plantation (1790)

With four miles of hard beach and the ocean as its eastern boundary, a 1,600-acre tract of land at the southeastern end of St. Simons Island surrounds the area where the Battle of Bloody Marsh was fought (1742). It was this property that was first granted to William McIntosh, who fought in that battle as a sixteen-year-old cadet and later served bravely in the American Revolution. The earliest records show this property as Kelvyn Grove, possibly named by McIntosh for a home in Scotland. It is unclear who named the plantation or just when the spelling changed to Kelvin Grove. What is known is that McIntosh sold the land to John Titus Morgan, who later sold it to Thomas Cater.

Sometime in 1798, Thomas Cater moved from Liberty County, Georgia, to St. Simons with his wife, Elizabeth Franklin, and their young son, Benjamin Franklin (Ben). Tragically, Thomas Cater was murdered at Kelvin Grove Plantation (c. 1808) by the overseer, who was having an affair with Elizabeth Cater.

The night Thomas Cater was killed, a faithful slave carried young Ben to Retreat Plantation, the home of Maj. William Page. As guardian, Major Page made sure that Ben was educated at Yale before he assumed charge of the Cater estate at Kelvin Grove Plantation.

Ben Cater married Anne Armstrong, who died giving birth to twins in 1835. One of the twins died and was buried with Anne. Sometime later Anne's sister Margaret, who had come to Kelvin Grove to care for the surviving twin, married Ben Cater. Named Anne Armstrong Cater for her mother, the lone-twin daughter was called Annie. She and her step-mother/aunt Margaret stayed on at Kelvin Grove after Ben Cater's death in 1839.

Annie Cater married James P. Postell, whose Charleston-based Huguenot family had left South Carolina to live in Savannah. After their marriage, the Postells lived at Kelvin Grove with Margaret Cater, who died in 1876. Annie Postell bore ten children, and the Kelvin Grove mansion resounded with happy noises of the large family. Two of these children appear in *The Beloved Invader*: James Mackbeth Postell (1856–1913), who was retarded from a childhood illness and died unmarried at age fifty-seven; and Clifford Hopkins Postell (1869–1945). The family participated actively as members of Christ Church, Frederica.

To Postell's credit, he returned to Kelvin Grove after the Civil War. The island had been evacuated, so he moved his family to Mt. Pleasant, Georgia, while he was away serving with the Confederacy. The pre-Civil War, two-storied Kelvin Grove was the only island home with a balcony commanding an ocean view. The house itself was built of tabby and surrounded on three sides by a twelve-foot-wide veranda.

At the close of the war, the Postells, along with "Ole Miss" (as the slaves called Margaret Cater), faced reconstruction of a very personal nature. The Kelvin Grove home was still standing but in such ruinous condition it had to be razed to make room for a new home.

Progressive, industrious "Captain Jim" not only rebuilt Kelvin Grove but he became the exuberant voice and personality that the island community needed in order to enter a different way of life. He encouraged tourism, offering his own four miles of beach property and an adjoining 150 acres as a development opportunity. Postell showed a supportive attitude toward the lumber mills at Gascoigne Bluff on the Frederica River by agreeing to survey and landscape for the owners.

Both before and after the war, James Postell was known as a gracious host, a prosperous planter of sea-island cotton, and an avid reader whose library included volumes of classic and scientific literature. Fascinated by conchology, Postell built a rare shell collection of more than six thousand varieties which was purchased by Roanoke College of Virginia in 1876. His contributions to museums were acknowledged as valuable natural history accessions.

James Postell died in 1898, and Annie Cater Postell died in 1911; they were buried at Christ Church Cemetery. During their lives they saw vast tracts of Kelvin Grove used as home sites for their children and others developed as ocean-front hotel property. The hotels included the St. Simons Hotel (c. 1888), which was located near present-day Massengale Park and burned in 1898, and the King and Prince Hotel development. The Battle of Bloody Marsh National Monument Park, the St. Simons airport, and the U.S. Coast Guard Station are also on Kelvin Grove land.

Orange Grove Plantation (1790)

Orange Grove Plantation was named for the great numbers of orange trees planted by its first owner. This island tract on Dunbar Creek south of Frederica was granted originally to John Terry, a silversmith and recorder of Frederica. Terry vacated the property, and the grant went to James Bruce of Savannah, who already owned a lot in the town of Frederica on the island. Bruce's daughter Rebecca married Maj. Samuel Wright (1790), and they moved to Orange Grove Plantation. Major Wright held commission in the Glynn County Militia Regiment, served several terms in the Georgia House of Representatives and Senate, and was Glynn County court justice from 1791 until his death in 1804.

Mary Wright, daughter of Samuel and Rebecca Bruce Wright, married George Abbott of Frederica on February 2, 1808. They lived at Rose Hill, her parents' house at Orange Grove Plantation. George Abbott had left Ireland in the late 1770s to open a mercantile business in Savannah. His marriage to Mary was performed by the Rev. Mr. Best and was the first wedding in the new parish of Christ Church, Frederica. Abbott was a founder of that church and laid the cornerstone in 1820.

In addition to the plantation, Abbott ran a thriving general store (c. 1807). Located on the narrow wharf at Frederica, Abbott's store was a gathering place, an information center. Abbott was the first postmaster once mail service to the island began around 1800.

Several of the Abbotts' children died as infants, and George died in 1825. Left with two daughters (Mary and Ellen), Mary wrote their Abbott kin in Dublin, Ireland, and asked for help with the plantation. George's younger brother, who had wanted to follow George when he first left home to start a mercantile business in the New World, was willing to oblige. With a small inheritance from his father's estate, Richard Abbott, his wife, Agnes (a native of Whitehaven, England), their young daughter, Deborah, and a nurse-maid (Mary Dunne) left Ireland to come to St. Simons (c. 1829).

Three years later, following the birth of a daughter, Ann, both Agnes Abbott and the children's nurse died of malaria fever. At Richard's death in 1836, Mary Wright Abbott ("Aunt Abbott") became legal guardian of Deborah (later married to Horace Bunch Gould, son of James and Janie Harris Gould) and Ann (later married to James Gowen, son of William and Mary Harrison Gowen).

Orange Grove had no sons to carry the Abbott name, and nothing remains of the house at Rose Hill. Today the property is part of the development known as Sea Palms West.

Cannon's Point Plantation (1793)

Cannon's Point Plantation was named for Daniel Cannon, master carpenter of Oglethorpe's Frederica. Cannon owned a land grant between the Hampton River and Jones Creek that covered the northeast end of St. Simons Island. The small cottage that Cannon had built for himself was still standing when John Couper bought the land for a homesite. Couper used the cottage to house the children's tutor, William Browne. John Fraser stayed at the cottage before his marriage to Couper's daughter, Anne. Overlooking the Hampton River, Cannon's Point offered a delightful view of Little St. Simons Island across the marshes.

Built about 1804, the plantation house of Rebecca Maxwell and John Couper at Cannon's Point was a three-storied mansion that exuded the hospitality of its owners. A wide veranda encompassed the spacious square home and included large porticos on either end. The English tabby basement was capped by upper floors of white clapboard with green shutters. People said the house took on the very warm, comfortable personality of John Couper himself. Couper was generous and jovial, loved children, and enjoyed guests. To add to his popularity with the other residents of St. Simons, this native Scot was an avid devotee of agricultural experimentation. Couper's Cannon's Point was lush with any vegetation he could induce to grow: long-staple sea-island cotton; sugar cane; date palms; olive, orange, and lemon trees; and an endless variety of flowers and vegetables all cultivated and perfected.

Of particular significance was that the giant live oak tree James Gould acquired for the sternpost carving on the first U.S. Navy ship came from Cannon's Point. Couper's blacksmith, Cuffy, welded an iron band for the stump, which was inscribed *U.S. Frigate Constitution, Seventeen Ninety-four.*

John Couper of Cannon's Point. (Courtesy of Merriam A. Bass)

John Couper arrived in Savannah, Georgia, from Scotland in 1775 when he was sixteen years old. His father, a Presbyterian minister in Lochwinnoch Parish near Glasgow, had three other sons, none of whom tried his patience like the mischievous red-haired, blue-eyed John. Young Couper's father well may have breathed a sigh of relief to see him (and his raucous sense of humor) leave for a life in the American colonies.

Couper apprenticed with an English firm in Savannah that relocated in St. Augustine, Florida, during the Revolutionary War. Afterwards he entered a business venture as a merchant in Sunbury (Liberty County, Georgia), where he also served as a justice.

In Sunbury, he met and married Rebecca Maxwell, whose Maxwell ancestors were a ruling family in Scotland. Becca, as John Couper called his tall, slender, aristocratic bride, had grown up near Midway on the plantation owned by her Scottish father James Maxwell. She longed to visit Caerlaverock Castle on the Firth of Solway in Scotland, which was the feudal domain of the titled Maxwells.

Rebecca Couper was known as a superb and gracious hostess, due in part to the perfection of Cannon's Point legendary chef, Sans Foix. His reputation was second only to Cupidon, master chef of the Marquis de Montalet at Sapelo Island. The plantation feasts were culinary delights, and the techniques were closely guarded secrets. Sans Foix never revealed how he could debone a whole turkey and, as if by magic, maintain the roasted bird's shape, a feat that amazed visiting dignitaries and brought squeals of delight from the children. There were waffles and tarts, wafers and scones, freshly prepared meats and vegetables of such variety and succulence as to be unsurpassed anywhere on the island. A picnic basket furnished by Sans Foix was a treasure befitting the warmth and ease of life at Cannon's Point.

Entertainment at the plantation always included the Scottish bagpipes mastered by Johnson the butler (also called "Fiddler Johnny"). At the insistence of John Couper, the plantation community sang and made cheerful merriment at their gatherings. Johnson would blow four long blasts into a giant conch shell to awaken the plantation; another signal on the conch shell announced arriving guests. "Fiddler Johnny" also performed at the serving of the meticulous meals readied by Sans Foix.

John and Rebecca Couper made a handsome couple. Sixteen years younger than John, Rebecca bore their five children: James Hamilton Couper was born in Sunbury and named for John's business partner, James Hamilton; Anne, John, Jr., Isabella, and William Audley were born at Cannon's Point. In addition to their own children the Coupers opened their home to the orphaned daughters of Thomas and Mary Dews Johnston of Savannah. In 1807 Ann Mary, thirteen, and Jane Elizabeth, twelve, came to live with their uncle John Couper, their father's relative from Scotland.

The children were taught at Cannon's Point until they were old enough to go away to school. In May 1803 William Browne, a British tutor from Oxford, came to St. Simons to teach the children of John Couper and Maj. William Page of Retreat Plantation. Browne arrived from Savannah on the schooner *York* and witnessed the Ebo (Island usage for Igbo) uprising at Dunbar Creek. Browne died on July 24, 1830, and is buried in the cemetery at Christ Church, Frederica.

John Couper owned as many as 130 slaves at one point, and he refused to permit branding or flogging, a firm position shared by his partner James Hamilton and by their friend Thomas Spalding of Sapelo Island. Weighing heavy on their minds was one group of Ebo slaves they imported, ten or twelve of whom preferred suicide by drowning to enslavement in a faraway land. Eugenia Price develops some of the survivors of that group of Ebo slaves into important supporting roles in her novels.

Big Boy, one of the Ebo slaves from West Africa who survived the tragic uprising at Dunbar Creek (May 1803), became John Couper's fisherman and a favorite of his daughter Anne. Couper gave Big Boy to Anne's husband, John Fraser, to serve as groom and fisherman for the young couple when they moved from England to settle on St. Simons Island. Couper also gave his daughter and son-in-law another of the Ebo slaves, June, and Anne's personal maid, Eve. Their story line complements and moves the plots of *Bright Captivity* and *Where Shadows Go*. It is Eve who knows Anne better than she knows herself and who brings about Anne's determination to mature and be stronger. Eve's husband June is responsible and loyal, helping John Fraser become a planter in his own right.

It was beyond comprehension the amount of energy John Couper placed into building the island's society. As a citizen of early Georgia, the well-loved Scot represented Glynn County in the 1798 convention that drew up the state constitution. His activities included serving as president in the Union Agricultural Society and the exclusive St. Andrews Society of Darien. Devoted to his faith, Couper was one of the first vestrymen of Christ Church, Frederica. His donation of land on the south end of the island (the government paid one dollar), made James Gould's dream, the building of a lighthouse, a reality. With all his popularity and prominence, the "best of all worlds" for John Couper and his family was their beloved Cannon's Point Plantation.

Eugenia Price has given prominence throughout the *St. Simons Trilogy* to the Coupers of Cannon's Point because of John Couper's influential role in the life of the island. To the delight of her readers, Price is developing her *Georgia Trilogy* around the Couper family,

Ruins of Cannon's Point Plantation, St. Simons Island. (Photograph © 1987 by David King Gleason)

children, and grandchildren. Her in-depth treatment parallels the prominent role each member of the family played through the years. Incidents that unfolded for James Gould and his descendants in the *St. Simons Trilogy* are examined in depth from the heart of the Cannon's Point master, John Couper. "Jock," who outlived his Becca by five years, was buried by her side at age ninety-one in Christ Church Cemetery in 1850.

Cannon's Point has belonged to the Sea Island Company since 1971. All that remain, following a fire at the turn of the century, are the chimneys and the great fireplace used by Sans Foix to prepare his famed confections and feasts. Of course the observant eye can spy vestiges of exotic blooms, date palms, and olive trees; and archeologists can unearth nearly a century's worth of evidence that John Couper was the host even the strong-minded abolitionist Fanny Kemble Butler found to be both charming and steadfast.

Hamilton Plantation (1793) and Hopeton Plantation/Altama (Altamaha River)

To continue our St. Simons chronology we must include at this point the emergence of Hamilton Plantation before examining the life and work of John Couper's descendants. After all, it was largely Couper's business partnership with James Hamilton that provided the earliest development of St. Simons and the Altamaha River area.

In 1793, James Hamilton—planter, shipper, and merchant—had to his credit the solid friendship of John Couper, a strong business acumen, and the insight to establish a wharf at his Gascoigne Bluff location. From there ships could transport the sea-island crops—cargoes of cotton and lumber—that would be sold in London and all over the world. This land first belonged to Captain Gascoigne, whose command of the sloop *Hawk* brought Oglethorpe and his British regiment to the island. It had passed from Gascoigne to Major Alexander Bissett and later to Richard Leake, who had grown cotton there since 1780, before Hamilton acquired it.

Hamilton lived on this valuable land part of the year, although his wide business interests required that he travel extensively. Like Couper,

James Hamilton was one of the first vestrymen of Christ Church, Frederica, and he contributed to the civic life of the island community and of Glynn County. He named his plantation home and tract Hamilton and developed his wharf and landing on the Frederica River into a shipping port that planters from the entire island could use.

Hamilton and Couper maintained their ties of friendship and business long after James Hamilton retired to Philadelphia. They had joint properties on the mainland near Brunswick. They owned a small island (called Carrs) on the Altamaha River and a 2,000-acre tract first granted by South Carolina to William Hopeton, Esq., in 1763. Hamilton and Couper cultivated the land but no home was built there until Couper's son became the owner. James Hamilton died in Philadelphia in 1829.

It was the children of John Couper who brought the Hamilton holdings to full fruition. Couper's oldest son, James Hamilton Couper, brought great honor and recognition to the two men whose name he bore. He managed to buy his father's interests in the partnership, and following his godfather's death, he maintained successful and profitable management for the Hamilton heirs.

James Hamilton Couper graduated from Yale with honors in 1814, took complete responsibility for Hopeton Plantation on the Altamaha by 1816, and in 1827 married sixteen-year-old Caroline Wylly, daughter of Alexander Wylly of St. Simons. James, always meticulous, methodical, and advanced for his age, was known as the "old gentleman" to his family and friends when he was just a boy.

There seemed no limit to young Couper's interests and abilities. Just as his father had extracted oil from olives, James invented a way to obtain oil from cotton seed. He experimented with microscopes before scientists in the universities had a good command of them. He studied abroad to perfect his ideas of crop rotation and the use of dikes. His architectural skills were so recognized that his design was used for Christ Church in Savannah. He kept such detailed daily records that water-color drawings illustrated even the more mundane of charts. His hobby of boat racing, like all his endeavors, came under his close supervision and improvement at each and every phase.

Young Caroline Wylly Couper made a home out of one of the cottages at Hopeton until her husband could complete his redesign of the huge tabby sugar house as a three-storied family mansion. Some forty years and eight children later, James designed a smaller home on the Hopeton property for their retirement (Altama, c. 1857). The old house at Hopeton was closed, and the cultivation responsibilities were passed to James' younger brother William Audley Couper, who with his wife, Hannah King of Retreat Plantation, had for some time been in charge of Hamilton Plantation at St. Simons.

Prior to that time Hamilton Plantation had been managed by James' brother-in-law John Fraser, the handsome British marine who was married to James' sister Anne, John Couper's oldest daughter. The *Georgia Trilogy* relates John and Anne Fraser's romantic story: initially they met during the British officer's occupation of Cumberland and St. Simons islands during the War of 1812, they courted, and they were married in 1816. The couple lived in London, and Anne was able to travel to Caerlaverock Castle, the ancestral Maxwell home in Scotland that her mother, Rebecca Maxwell, had longed to visit. They returned to St. Simons to live at Lawrence Plantation adjoining Cannon's Point.

Lawrence Plantation (1801)

Originally granted to John Lawrence of Frederica, Lawrence Plantation had a series of owners until John Couper purchased it in 1801. Managing the plantation as one of his cotton-producing holdings, Couper gave Lawrence to Ann and John Fraser when they moved to St. Simons from England. The couple had spent several years with John's father, James Fraser, in London. Lawrence was a tougher challenge for John Fraser than the years of gallant military life he cherished and upon which he thrived. It had never occurred to him that he would ever become a planter or own slaves. But the British military had few active commissions—in fact none for him.

Fraser's love for Anne Couper and her overwhelming sense of home and belonging compelled him to want whatever she wanted and therefore to accept John Couper's offer of Lawrence Plantation. There, in the late 1820s, John Fraser more than proved his ability to be a planter. His willingness to learn and to excel won him the respect of the other island planters, but, most important, of Anne Couper's father and brother. Fraser showed an aptitude for selecting cotton seeds and for the regimen required in bringing forth the most profitable crops possible.

James Couper eventually trusted Fraser with the responsibility of Hamilton Plantation. The Frasers moved from their small farmhouse at Lawrence into the much larger colonial home with lattice foundations that overlooked the Frederica River and marshes. They were happy to have more room for their growing family, but a certain nostalgia about their years at Lawrence, near Cannon's Point, drew Anne back there when John Fraser died in July 1839. The Lawrence property is owned today by the Sea Island Company.

In her afterword to *Where Shadows Go*, Eugenia Price walks her readers through the cemetery at Christ Church, Frederica, as though they were the graves of her own family members. The death of John Fraser was one of the most difficult to work through for Price, and she made no effort to hide that emotion from her readers. You will learn from her that John Fraser's father is buried there, along with John's brother, Dr. William Fraser, and his family. Price's recurrent theme of finding a sense of place was a strong one for the Frasers as each brother fell in love with the very people whose homes they were sent to capture. The War of 1812 brought John and William Fraser to Georgia—the women they loved kept them there. John, of course, had married Anne Couper; William married Frances Wylly of the Village Plantation and established himself as a prominent doctor in Darien before John brought his family back to Georgia.

It was a happy reunion when sometime later John and William welcomed their father, James Fraser, to America. Father Fraser's health was poor, and he spent his final days with William. "Jock" Couper was a special friend to James Fraser. Their mutual ties to Scotland bound them in one way, but their shared love of family and their adopted St. Simons Island gave their relationship meaning and depth.

Retreat Plantation (1802)

Anna Matilda Page, Anne Couper Fraser's best friend from early childhood, lived at Retreat Plantation. She was born in 1798 at Hampton Plantation while her parents, Maj. William Page and Hannah Timmons, were there visiting a friend and fellow South Carolinian, Maj. Pierce Butler. The Pages decided to make St. Simons their home and leased a residence and property on the southwestern tip of St. Simons Island bordering the Frederica River and reaching to Gascoigne Bluff.

The eighteenth-century English-style cottage had been built as a replica of Orange Hall, Oglethorpe's home at Frederica. It was designed as a first dwelling for Thomas Spalding and Sarah Leake, as Spalding's parents, James and Margery McIntosh Spalding, had been living at Orange Hall when Thomas was born. James Spalding, who had come to America in 1760, and his business partner Donald MacKay owned a successful mercantile company. MacKay and Spalding operated Indian trading posts from a central warehouse at Frederica, but they lost the business due to the Revolutionary War. Spalding regained his fortune as a successful planter of long-staple cotton and became one of Glynn County's largest landowners. His son Thomas eventually owned most of Sapelo Island, where he became known as the "Laird of Sapelo."

In 1802, Thomas Spalding sold his St. Simons property to Major Page, who named it Retreat Plantation. This property overlooked the sound and had a view of Jekyll Island. As the Pages had only one child, the original Spalding home was comfortable for them. Major Page purchased the adjoining Newfield tract and concentrated his energies into making Retreat Plantation one of the four largest and most prosperous cotton plantations on the island. It was a business establishment in every sense, and the Page's daughter, Anna Matilda, learned the management of the plantation in addition to receiving a fine cultural education.

An important part of her education was domestic training from her mother, French lessons from Mrs. Henri duBignon (Jekyll Island), and literary discipline from William Browne, the tutor John

Couper brought from England in 1803 to run a school for the children at Cannon's Point. Daily lessons at Cannon's Point meant a horseback ride of twelve miles each way from Retreat to the north end of the island for Anna Matilda and a trusted slave.

While Major Page was away on his many travels, Anna Matilda supervised every need of the giant plantation with skills that were a complement to her parents. She took her place in society as a true "Southern belle" and was formally introduced by a coming-out ball in her honor at the Savannah West Broad Street mansion of her father's friend William Scarbrough (see also part 3).

It is widely believed that the charming young girl (called "Sweet Ann Page" by her father) convinced British admiral Sir George Cockburn not to damage her beloved Retreat when the English Navy invaded the coast of Georgia in 1815. It was during that same occupation of the coastal islands that British naval officers John and William Fraser entered a realm that would root their futures in Georgia, not England. Although *Bright Captivity* refers to the capture of Anne Couper by Lt. John Fraser while she, her family, and Anna Matilda Page were at a house party on Cumberland Island, Eugenia Price reveals the captivity of more than one heart in the closing days of that final war with England.

Of her many beaus, Anna Matilda chose to marry Thomas Butler King of Kingston, Massachusetts, the son of Daniel and Hannah Lord King. Within two years of their wedding in 1824, both of Anna Matilda's parents died and she inherited Retreat with all its beauty and responsibility. She was as well prepared as any young woman of her day, and in tandem with her husband's advancing political career, Anna Matilda King successfully managed to be wife, mother, and overseer of all the plantation's business.

In *Where Shadows Go*, Thomas Butler King was away when their firstborn son, William, contracted a fever and died. The island families mourned with Anna Matilda, especially Anne Fraser and her children. For a time after William's death, the Kings lived on one of their mainland plantations, Waverly, near Kingsland, Georgia. They eventually lost most of their mainland property and settled permanently at Retreat on St. Simons.

The son of a Massachusetts statesman, King served in the Georgia Senate (1832–35, 1837–38) and the U.S. Congress (1839–41). He successfully pushed for passage of a bill to establish a Home Squadron by the Navy, the organization that became the North Atlantic Squadron (1890s), the Atlantic Fleet (1900s), and finally the present-day United States Fleet.

A pioneer in the development of railroads, King was instrumental in establishing the Brunswick and Altamaha Canal. A state charter had been granted in the late 1820s to the Brunswick Canal Company for the construction of a canal that would connect the Altamaha and Turtle rivers. This would give inland access to the port at Brunswick. The project was abandoned because of financial trouble. In the 1830s Thomas Butler King reorganized with capital from Boston investors. A new charter was extended to the Brunswick Canal and Railroad

Ruins at Retreat Plantation, St. Simons Island. (Courtesy of Merriam A. Bass)

Company. When investors withdrew their money in the panic of 1837, King involved his fellow islanders in funding and managing the project. The Canal opened June 1, 1854.

The Kings' vast household of nine children, slaves, and visitors was expanded by outbuildings. There was a guest house, a dormitory for the boys they called "Grasshopper Hall," hothouses, a school, a hospital, tabby barns and servant's quarters, and the fabled four-storied cotton house, a light from which guided ships in the days before James Gould built his lighthouse.

Anna Matilda not only managed a vast household and a giant plantation's business, she also somehow found the time and energy to nurture and cultivate the rare flowers, shrubs, and plants that she loved. Because of her expertise, this plantation was known for its remarkable efficiency, the beauty of its formal gardens, and the magnificent approach to its grounds through an avenue of live oaks. What a happy scene of dances, houseparties, and other activities graced Retreat Plantation.

Then, as if a foreshadow of the war years, in 1859 sadness loomed over their existence. Death claimed Butler, the oldest surviving son, followed shortly by a death that took away the heartbeat of the great plantation, Anna Matilda King herself. War was soon declared, and Thomas Butler King saw his remaining sons join the Confederacy, one never to return. King served the South as an emissary to Europe from 1861 to 1863, but his health failed and in 1864 he, too, died and was buried at Christ Church cemetery.

Legendary is the story of Neptune Small, the faithful servant who carried the slain young Lord King from the blood-soaked fields at the Battle of Fredericksburg all the way home to Retreat. As if he could not rest, Neptune Small ventured back to the battlefield of Virginia to find another King son, "Tip" (R. Cuyler King), bringing him home safely.

The Kings' daughter Hannah, who married William Audley Couper, lived at Hamilton Plantation while her husband managed the property for his brother, James Hamilton Couper. After the Civil War, one of the surviving King sons, Mallery, and his wife, Eugenia Grant of Elizafield Plantation (granddaughter of Dr. and Mrs. Robert

Grant of Oatlands Plantation, St. Simons), lived at Retreat with their three young daughters, Mary Anna, Frances Buford, and Florence Page. They found it impossible to recover the family's great losses both at Retreat and at Elizafield, so eventually they left.

The historic house at Retreat burned, as did the cotton house, but the old tabby barn is now the remodeled clubhouse for the Sea Island Golf Course. There are ruins to see—a slave burying ground and the avenue of ancient live oaks to a breathless view of the sound and Jekyll Island across the way. Eugenia Price filters the pages of her novels with memorable glimpses of Retreat—the names Spalding, Page, and King belong to real people who move along the shell-covered walks and the moss-draped lanes as mystically as Price's descriptions of island light and shadows.

Oatlands Plantation (Early 1800s) and Elizafield/Grantly/Evelyn Plantations (Altamaha River)

Dr. Robert Grant, a prominent physician and rice planter and a native of Scotland, made his home first in South Carolina and then settled in the Altamaha River area of Georgia. Dr. Grant and his wife, Sarah Foxworth, held property on the Altamaha River that was divided into three parts: they and their families lived at Elizafield (named for Dr. Grant's mother in Scotland), and they cultivated Grantly and Evelyn plantations in rice, cotton, and sugar cane. The latter two plantations also housed slaves who worked the fields.

Oatlands Plantation was the Grant summer home at St. Simons. The property was south of Lawrence Plantation and belonged first to James Bruce, whose daughters, Rebecca and Elizabeth, sold it to James Harrison in 1788. Sometime in the early 1800s, Dr. Robert Grant bought Oatlands, and he and Sarah retired there around 1834, giving Elizafield to their son Hugh Fraser Grant. Dr. Grant was a warden and organizer of Christ Church, Frederica, in 1808 and became active in the community life on St. Simons. He died at age eighty-one, after which his wife lived at Elizafield with Hugh and his family.

Other planters and great rice plantations were established in the Darien area. The Grants' neighbors along the Altamaha were

Maj. Pierce Butler at Butler Island Plantation; John Couper and James Hamilton, along the south branch of the Altamaha, who were business partners and co-owners of Hopeton Plantation; Dr. Grant's plantations below Hopeton (Elizafield, Grantly, and Evelyn); and William Brailsford's Broadfield and New Hope, which were adjacent to Dr. Grant.

Today Oatlands is privately owned, and the tabby ruins of Dr. Grant's home are still standing. As for Elizafield, part of it became a park of the State of Georgia, and a portion was dedicated for the establishment of Boys Estate (much like the famous Boys Town in Nebraska). In 1976 the institution became Youth Estate for both boys and girls.

St. Clair/Village Plantation (Early 1800s)

As Loyalist supporters of the British Crown, the William Armstrong family removed to the Bahamas during the Revolutionary War. William and Ann Armstrong's youngest daughter, Margaret, married Alexander Campbell Wylly (St. Clair/Village Plantation), and their granddaughter Anne (Margaret's niece) married Benjamin Franklin Cater (Kelvin Grove Plantation). Anne Cater died in childbirth, and her sister Margaret (named for her Aunt Margaret Wylly) later married Ben Cater.

After the death of William, Ann Armstrong left the Bahamas and lived with the Wyllys, her daughter Margaret's family, in the old St. Clair house until her death at age eighty-two in 1816. A sago palm was planted by her grave at Christ Church cemetery, as she was credited with bringing the plant to St. Simons Island. A sago palm still grows in the churchyard near the Armstrong burial plot.

The St. Clair property was granted to Archibald Sinclair during Oglethorpe's time and was a successful plantation as early at 1745. By 1755 the land was vacated and granted in 1765 to Donald Forbes, who sold it to Lachlan McIntosh. Maj. William McIntosh, a son, lived there and died in 1799. Maj. Pierce Butler bought the land and house as an investment, reselling to Capt. Alexander Wylly for an addition to Wylly's Village Plantation. The Wylly family lived there for a time.

The Wylly's daughter Frances and her husband, Dr. William Fraser, lived at St. Clair before moving to Darien. Dr. Fraser, who had come to St. Simons from England as a naval officer during the War of 1812, became mayor of Darien.

In the early 1830s the St. Clair Club, known for its fine dinner meetings, and the St. Simons Agricultural and Sporting Club used the large, rambling home as a clubhouse. The plantation house at St. Clair burned in 1857.

Captain Wylly's Village Plantation encompassed more than a thousand acres. A native of Savannah, Wylly had attended school at Oxford and was a Loyalist during the Revolution. He was a British army officer and lived in the Bahamas following the war. There he met and married Margaret Armstrong, had four children, and then brought his family to Jekyll Island. The couple had three more children at Jekyll. Soon Captain Wylly was able to purchase the St. Clair property and move his large family to St. Simons. The youngest Wylly daughter, Caroline, was born at St. Clair.

The addition of more land—once a Salzburger settlement known as German Village—enabled Wylly to remodel an existing dwelling, move from the St. Clair house, and establish his property as Village Plantation. His new home was a roomy and richly appointed farmhouse that afforded a view of Long Island and, a mile to the east, the Atlantic Ocean.

Family, friends, and visiting relatives packed into the lovely home to celebrate the 1827 Christmas-night wedding of sixteen-year-old Caroline Wylly to John Couper's oldest son, James Hamilton Couper (by then thirty-three). The week-long house party culminated in a wedding supper that all the island families attended. After a sumptuous feast, the gathering toasted the bride and groom and saw them depart for Cannon's Point, from which they would leave the next morning for their new home, Hopeton Plantation on the Altamaha River.

The years that followed would hold an ample amount of sadness for the family at the Village. The deaths of the oldest Wylly daughter, Susan (1829), and Captain Wylly (1833) somewhat overshadowed the marriage of the oldest son, Alexander William, to

Sarah Spalding, the daughter of the Thomas Spaldings of Sapelo Island. In the summer of 1837 Dr. William Fraser, husband of Frances Anne Wylly, did not live long enough to reach Saratoga Springs and treatments for heart failure. Before Fraser's body could be brought home for burial, a devastating hurricane severely damaged the Georgia coast.

December 1838 brought more tragedy. Young John Wylly was shot to death by Dr. Thomas Hazzard of Pike's Bluff. An unsolved property dispute over a boundary had festered between the two families to such a point that many islanders feared such a calamity. Even though it was December, in *New Moon Rising* Eugenia Price knew to mention the "deep pink camellias" blooming next to Mrs. Wylly's bushes the day of John's funeral. "There was never a season on St. Simons Island when nothing grew, nothing budded, nothing bloomed. Death came often to its people, but never to the land."

By February a broken column set on a square base of pinkish marble was inscribed as follows:

Sacred
to the memory of
John Armstrong Wylly
who fell a victim
to his
generous courage
on the 3rd of December, 1838
Age 32 years and 1 month

The marker stands today in the cemetery at Christ Church, Frederica.

Eugenia Price offers moving accounts of this tragedy, and its effect on the families involved, in both *New Moon Rising* and *Where Shadows Go*. One of Price's foremost talents in writing is her sensitive treatment of sorrow, loss, and catastrophic events. She portrays the strengths her characters exhibit from their faith in God with such honesty, empathy, and warmth that a kinship develops between the author, the reader, and the people involved.

An outstanding example of this merging of emotions is Price's treatment of the sinking of the steamship *Pulaski*. In June of 1838, the summer before John Wylly was killed, this frightening episode at sea pulled at the hearts of the island community. Frances Wylly Fraser, who had mourned for her husband in the year since his death, was persuaded by family to take an outing on the *Pulaski*. Her sister Caroline's husband, James Hamilton Couper, would be sailing on business and would escort her and her small son, Menzies. Their good friend Mrs. Nightingale, from Dungeness on Cumberland Island, and her infant daughter, Louisa, would be in their group. While out at sea, the *Pulaski's* boilers exploded, but the ever methodical James Couper, through quick thinking, was able to rescue himself and all in his care. Tragically, 77 of 131 passengers died.

In *Where Shadows Go*, Price unveils the accident through the Wylly/Fraser/Couper families, while in the *Savannah Quartet* she devotes an entire novel (*To See Your Face Again*) to the Savannah passengers and the aftereffects of such a catastrophic event. Couper's true, handwritten account is among the archival treasures Price used for each of the novels. The story and the people are the same. The central event doesn't change in its telling whether it affects (among many others) the Middleton/Rutledge/Pinckney families of Charleston, the Bryan/Mackay/Browning families of Savannah, or the Wylly/Couper/Fraser families of St. Simons Island. What changes is family members' viewpoint on the accident—from a great sense of loss to an overwhelming relief, depending on whether they had to mourn a death or could welcome back a fortunate survivor. Part of Eugenia Price's style that readers have grown to love is her masterful ability to retell such events with a poignant complexity of perspective.

After 1838, Mrs. Wylly remained with her daughters at Village Plantation until her death in 1850. Eugenia Price portrays one unmarried daughter, Heriot, with special gentleness and insight. Heriot was an eccentric loner who loved the outdoors and every phase of natural beauty found on the island. She becomes a memorable character—one who fearlessly darts in and out of lives to make her own unique contribution to the story.

A portion of the Wylly holdings along Village Creek became the Reynolds-Bagley family retreat in 1938. This exclusive, part-time hideaway was named Musgrove for the legendary half-Indian Princess Mary Musgrove who had served as Oglethorpe's interpreter to the Indians. Musgrove Plantation was unknown to the public sector until 1976, when President-elect Jimmy Carter held his pre-inaugural cabinet meeting there.

West Point Plantation (1818) and Pike's Bluff Plantation (1827)

In 1818 South Carolinian Col. William Wigg Hazzard purchased the property known as West Point. Just north of Frederica, this land previously had passed from Donald MacKay to James Spalding to Lachlan McIntosh. The adjoining acreage to its north, used by Oglethorpe as a sentry station, was known as Pike's Bluff. The rector at Christ Church, Edmund Matthews, owned the land until his death in 1827, when his estate was sold to the Hazzard family. Dr. Thomas Fuller Hazzard, the colonel's younger brother, made his home there.

At the time John Wylly was killed over a boundary dispute by Dr. Thomas Hazzard (1838), the owners of West Point and Pike's Bluff were well-respected, integral parts of the island community. Active sportsmen, able writers, and devoted officers of Christ Church, each of the Hazzard brothers also served terms in the state legislature. Dr. Hazzard was not convicted of the charges of aggravated manslaughter, a decision that divided the tightly knit islanders. After Dr. Hazzard's death, Col. Hazzard bought his brother's land and maintained the two plantations as one estate.

Today Pike's Bluff is owned by the Sea Island Company. The large frame house at West Point has disappeared, but some ruins of tabby slave cabins remain. A large portion of West Point was sold for residential use except for a small section included in the Fort Frederica National Monument.

New St. Clair Plantation/Rosemount (1816) and Black Banks Plantation (1831)

In *Lighthouse*, after James Gould completed his surveying job

(c. 1796), he accepted a government contract to supervise the procurement of timber in Spanish East Florida. He built a cabin on the St. Marys River at the Mills Ferry tract owned by John McQueen (*see* Part 2). When Gould learned of his mother's death, he decided to settle permanently in the South. James's favorite sister, Mary, who corresponded with him faithfully, married a Mr. Gaylord she met while visiting their sister Rachel and her husband, John Trowbridge, in Utica, New York. Their brother Horace and his wife, Jessie, continued to live in Bangor in the house James built. They were with Kate Gould when she died.

James met and fell in love with Jane (Janie) Harris while he was on a business trip to Charleston in 1802. Her English parents, Mary and John Hartley Harris, had located first in Nassau, New Providence, in 1785 and later migrated to South Carolina around 1798. Her father, a former British army officer, had retired early due to ill health and had worked as a schoolmaster. When Gould met the family, Janie's siblings included Elizabeth, John Mackay (12), Charles (9), Stephen (4), and Caroline (an infant). Elizabeth had married a prosperous British officer, Capt. Samuel Bunch, and Jane had lived with them at the Bunch plantation in Nassau her last year there.

By 1805 Janie's father had moved the Harris family to Savannah so he could accept a position as schoolmaster arranged by his nephew, Charles Harris, mayor of Savannah. John and Mary Harris and their two oldest sons, John Mackay and Charles, died by the end of 1812.

After Samuel Bunch lost all his inheritance on his cotton plantation in Nassau, he and Elizabeth moved to Savannah to live with the Harris family. The Bunches cared for the younger children in the home James Gould bought for them—the Hampton-Lillibridge house in Savannah (*see* part 3). Later Captain Bunch became a cotton factor, tried and failed at several business ventures, sold real estate on the side, and at his death in 1816 was deeply in debt.

James and Janie married the year after they met and settled at Mills Ferry until 1807, when an Indian uprising forced their removal to Savannah. While there James learned that the government was accepting bids for the construction of a lighthouse and keeper's cottage on St. Simons Island. Just when all seemed lost he would get the chance to realize his lifelong goal.

Gould's design called for the tower to be tapered, octagonal, and 75 feet high from the foundation to the base of the iron lantern. The lantern (also octagonal) would be 10 feet high and would hold oil lamps suspended on chains. Work was completed by 1810, and President James Madison commissioned the lighthouse in 1811.

Gould was the first keeper, a position he held for twenty-seven years. He had built the keeper's cottage according to the government specifications (adjacent to the lighthouse), knowing it would mean cramped quarters for his growing family: James III (Jim, b. 1807), Mary (b. 1809), and Horace Bunch (b. 1812). Daughter Jane was born in 1817 at New St. Clair Plantation.

Until the War of 1812 ended, James Gould was only able to lease land for cultivation. The first St. Simons property that he purchased was a 900-acre tract from the post-Revolution confiscated estate of Maj. Samuel Wright. Gould's plantation, New St. Clair, was planted in sea-island cotton and reached across the center of the island from the Black Banks River to Dunbar Creek.

The center portion of the spacious brick-and-tabby plantation house had two stories with a one-story wing on each side. The house was built on a slight rise, and a profusion and variety of roses graced the sloping grounds. With Mary Gould's avid interest in the cultivation of roses, their house came to be called Rosemount.

Janie Gould's health required her to spend some time in Savannah. Early in 1820 she had regained her health, but she died suddenly of pneumonia after the great Savannah fire on January 11 of that year. James Gould's true "light" was gone, and she was buried in Savannah before he could reach her. When Christ Church, Frederica, was built that same year, James Gould was one of the first wardens.

James Gould made sure that his children were schooled properly. They were tutored on the island while young but were sent away for their higher education—the sons to prep school in New Haven, Connecticut, and college at Yale; the daughters to the Moravian Seminary in Bethlehem, Pennsylvania. Jim, the oldest, graduated from Yale and married the daughter of a hotel owner. Horace and more than forty others of his class of 1832 were dismissed two years before graduating for involvement in a student protest. *New Moon Rising* portrays Horace's coming to maturity and the events surrounding the Gould family through the close of the Civil War.

James Gould had purchased more than six hundred additional acres adjoining his New St. Clair Plantation to the south. This land, which he called Black Banks Plantation, had belonged to Oglethorpe's Col. John Graham before the Revolution. Gould gave ninety acres of the property to his son Jim to induce him to live at St. Simons. Jim accepted his father's offer and built a beautiful two-and-a-half-story tabby house with a columned piazza (c. 1832). Connecticut-born Alice Gould, Jim's unhappy wife, caused him eventually to return to the North with her and their son, Jamie. After they left the island, Jim sold Black Banks to his brother Horace, who had married Deborah Abbott of Orange Grove Plantation.

James Gould, who suffered from rheumatic gout, was unable to work as keeper of the light after 1837. With the loyal help of his daughter Mary, the cotton plantations continued to prosper for many years. James also remained an active supporter of Christ Church. At the time of his death in 1852, his younger daughter Jane (who lived until 1883) already was married to a wealthy merchant, Orville Richardson, of Baltimore. Gould left the ownership and management of New St. Clair and Rosemount in the devoted, capable hands of Mary Gould. She had never married, and many believed she had been in love with John Wylly at the time he was shot and killed by Dr. Thomas Hazzard.

Horace Bunch and Deborah Abbott Gould had ten children, all of whom survived well into their adult years. That a whole brood of siblings lived through their childhood was quite an uncommon occurrence in those days of malaria and inadequate medical knowledge.

The Goulds' first child, Jane (or Jennie as they called her), was born in 1846 at Black Banks Plantation. Horace and Deborah lived there as caretakers for Jim for a short time before Horace accepted a job on Blythe Island, an area west of Brunswick, between the Turtle and South Brunswick rivers. Through the late 1840s, Horace worked at Black Banks as superintendent on the run-down plantation of an absentee owner. Their second child, Jessie Caroline, was born at the plantation in 1848. By 1849 Jim definitely had decided to sell Black Banks to Horace. Six more children were born during the happy, prosperous years at Black Banks before the Civil War: Elizabeth Fraser (Lizzie, b. 1850); Horace Abbott (b. 1852); Mary Frances (May, b. 1854); Anna Deborah (b. 1857); James Dunn (Jimmy, b. 1859); and Helen Richardson (b. 1861).

In *New Moon Rising*, when Confederate officers ordered the evacuation of St. Simons in 1861, Mary Gould desperately clung to Rosemount. Her brother Horace made her leave after he rented a small furnished house in Blackshear, Georgia. The house was large enough only for Mary, their Aunt Caroline Harris, and the elderly slave couple Maum Larney and Papa John, who had been with the family since they lived on the St. Marys River. Blackshear, in Pierce

Anna Deborah Gould Dodge, second wife of Rev. Anson Dodge. (Courtesy of the Coastal Georgia Historical Society)

County, hopefully would be far enough inland for them to be safe.

A small, cramped cottage in Burneyville was refuge for Horace, Deborah, and their family (eight children by that time). Early in 1863 a ninth child was born, Angela La Coste (Angé). Horace received orders soon afterwards to report to the Confederacy; he would have to fight although he was in his mid-forties and the father of nine children.

In 1864, after serving as captain at the siege of Atlanta under the command of Confederate general Joseph E. (Joe) Johnston, Horace spent a short time on leave in Burneyville. In January 1865 Deborah named their tenth child, Joe, in honor of her favorite general. Horace managed to join his command in Savannah, delayed only by a wound he had received. They evacuated with the last troops before the pontoon bridge was destroyed and the city surrendered to Sherman.

On returning to the island, Horace was particularly anguished to discover that the octagonal lighthouse his father had designed and built was no more. Confederate soldiers were ordered to blow it up when they evacuated in 1862. Their superiors had feared that the St. Simons Light would easily guide Federal blockaders.

New St. Clair was also destroyed during the war, just as Mary Gould had feared, but Horace managed to buy back the plantation and house at Black Banks. Everything Mary Gould owned was gone, so she stayed with her father's Utica, New York, relatives for a time after the war. When Aunt Caroline died in 1870, Mary returned to the island for the last two years of her life. She repaired and lived in Maum Larney's old cabin at New St. Clair. Although Rosemount had been burned to the ground, some varieties of Mary's roses survived. One other rose remains today—the one Horace had carved on the stone that marks Mary's grave in Christ Churchyard.

After Horace died in 1881, Deborah lived on at Black Banks surrounded by children and grandchildren. She enjoyed several extended trips to visit with those who had moved away from the island, but her last four years, until her death in 1906, were spent at Black Banks, where she and Horace had always been happiest.

Residential development now covers most of the former New St.

Horace Bunch Gould of Black Banks Plantation. (Courtesy of the Coastal Georgia Historical Society)

Clair and Black Banks plantations. Sea Palms Golf and Country Club is on part of New St. Clair land; on Black Banks acreage is a subdivision that carries its name, with only a portion of Black Banks still owned by Gould descendants.

Map 4. St. Simons Island/Jekyll Island–Points of Interest

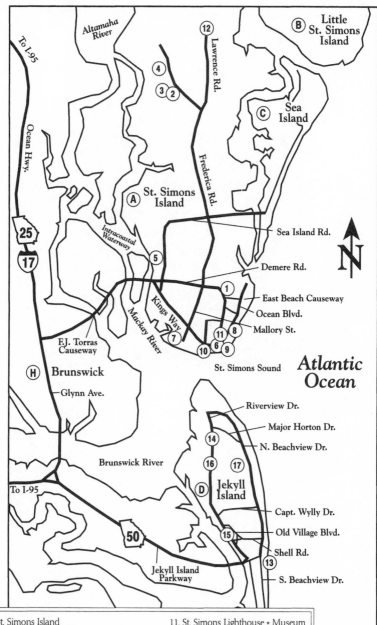

A. St. Simons Island
1. Bloody Marsh Battle Site
2. Christ Church, Frederica
3. Christ Church Cemetery
4. Fort Frederica
5. Gascoigne Bluff * Epworth-by-the-Sea
6. Neptune Park
7. Retreat Plantation
8. St. Simons Beach * Massengale Park
9. St. Simons Chamber of Commerce
10. St. Simons Fishing Pier

11. St. Simons Lighthouse * Museum
   of Coastal History
12. Taylor's Fish Camp
B. Little St. Simons Island
C. Sea Island (Long Island)
D. Jekyll Island
13. Convention Center
14. duBignon House Ruins
15. Jekyll Island Museum
16. Horton House Ruins
17. Millionaires Golf Course

Chapter 3

Points of Interest

G olden Isles, Georgia: A term most often applied to the islands of St. Simons, Little St. Simons, Sea Island, and Jekyll; accessible only from Brunswick, Georgia.

A. St. Simons Island

The essence of sea-island charm and natural beauty, St. Simons Island is central to the Eugenia Price *St. Simons* and *Georgia* trilogies. The island is reached by way of the Torras Causeway off U.S. Highway 17 at Brunswick, Georgia. Approaching from the north or the south on I-95, you will find well-marked exits showing the way to this popular destination—one of Georgia's largest barrier islands. Residential and resort areas alike bear the names of long-ago plantations, and even the most casual drive or walk becomes memorable, particularly for Eugenia Price readers. Her vivid descriptions of the marshes; the deep, dark woods; the light and the shadows; the churchyard, fort, and lighthouse—all of her word-pictures will flood your senses at once, and you will know you are at home.

Areas you will want to visit on St. Simons Island include:

1. Bloody Marsh Battle Site

A marker on today's Demere Road tells of the significant 1742 ambush and victory over the Spanish by Oglethorpe's British Regulars, his Indian allies, and the Scottish Highland Rangers from Darien. Located in the marshes along the old Military Road from Fort St. Simons on the south to Fort Frederica at the north, this property later became part of Kelvin Grove Plantation. A new historical marker on Frederica Road indicates the site of the strategic skirmish at Gully Hole Creek.

2. Christ Church, Frederica

Although the original church was founded in the chapel within the walls of Fort Frederica, the current structure on Frederica Road was erected in 1884 by Anson Green Phelps Dodge, Jr., as a memorial to his first wife, Ellen. It was on this site that Charles and John Wesley conducted their first services in the New World under the oak trees in 1736. The original 1820 building was damaged extensively during the Civil War.

3. Christ Church Cemetery

The cemetery is on the same property as the sanctuary. The oldest apparent gravestone date is 1803, but earlier gravesites are believed to exist. A walk through this churchyard is a veritable roll call of St. Simons colonists and planters and all those who have followed them. Journey into the island's heart and you can imagine hearing many sounds: steady murmurs of adults under moss-draped live oak trees sharing news of the day; cheerful voices of children playing on the grounds; sporadic shouts of soldiers and Indians in various brogues and languages; excited bursts of rhetoric amid the quiet prayers of priests and missionaries and evangelists; melodious songs of faith in mysterious African rhythms; and grief-filled sobs broken only by the crisp call of the painted bunting or the thunderous hammering of the great Lord God Bird (pileated woodpecker) far into the deep, dark woods of yesterday.

Rev. Anson G. P. Dodge family plot at Christ Churchyard, Frederica. Left to right: *graves of Anna Gould Dodge; Anson G. P. Dodge III; Rebecca Grew Dodge; and, in a joint grave, as specified in his will, Reverend Dodge and Ellen Ada Phelps Dodge. (Courtesy of Merriam A. Bass)*

4. Fort Frederica

This landmark on Frederica Road was the most expensive fort the British built in this country. Constructed in 1726 by Gen. James Edward Oglethorpe as an outpost and a defense of Savannah, Fort Frederica is now a national monument. Open daily, films are shown every half hour year-round. Informative talks and escorted tours are available in May through October, during which guests may see the carefully excavated foundations of the old town.

5. Gascoigne Bluff ❖ Epworth–by–the–Sea

Island terminus of the 1924 Torras Causeway, this property has always been the gateway to St. Simons Island. On this site are two tabby slave cabins that served as quarters on Hamilton Plantation. They are owned and used by Cassina Garden Club. Live oak timbers for the USS *Constitution* ("Old Ironsides") were cut and loaded here by James Gould (c. 1794). The upper part of the bluff is now a Methodist conference center, Epworth-by-the-Sea. Built in 1949 on the site of Hamilton Plantation, the center houses a museum that contains items from plantation days as well as artifacts from the Dodge-Meigs lumber mill. The museum focuses on the history of the Southern Methodist Conference. Admission is free.

6. Neptune Park

A public library is housed in the Old Casino Building, as is a theater where the Island Players give performances. The New Casino Building holds meeting rooms, a bowling alley, and a swimming pool (seasonal). There also is a playground and a park.

7. Retreat Plantation

Located across from Jekyll Island on Kings Way, this site is now part of Sea Island Golf Course. Retreat Plantation produced sea-island cotton, a superior quality cotton that made St. Simons famous and the plantation owners wealthy. Ruins of a slave hospital can still be seen, and the present clubhouse was formerly one of the plantation buildings. Retreat was owned by the Spaldings, who sold it to Maj. William Page. The only heir, Anna Matilda Page, married Thomas Butler King and lived at Retreat during its grandest days. An avenue of live oaks welcomes visitors.

8. St. Simons Beach ❖ Massengale Park

Several miles of fine-sand beaches run south and north of the Coast Guard Station. Picnic areas, parking, and bathing facilities are available.

9. St. Simons Chamber of Commerce

This is the island's information and welcome center. Details about St. Simons activities, overnight accommodations, and facilities are available here.

10. St. Simons Fishing Pier

Visitors arrived at this pier from the mainland in the days of the ferry boats. Both local people and visitors fish here. Nearby shopping and dining make this area as convenient as it is interesting.

St. Simons lighthouse and keeper's cottage, now the Museum of Coastal History
(Courtesy of the Coastal Georgia Historical Society; photograph by Merriam A. Bass)

11. St. Simons Lighthouse ❖ Museum of Coastal History

The present lighthouse was built in 1872, along with the lighthouse keeper's home. The fine old brick house and light replaced the original structures designed and built by James Gould in 1811. The first lighthouse was destroyed in 1862 during the Civil War. Maintained by the Coast Guard, the lighthouse is one of the oldest working lights in the country. The museum of the Coastal Georgia Historical Society is in the keeper's cottage. Its nine rooms have Georgia heart-of-pine floors, and the construction is of Savannah gray brick. Hours vary with the seasons.

12. Taylor's Fish Camp

Charter boats are available for fishing or just enjoying the island along the Hampton River near the sites of Cannon's Point and Lawrence plantations. Located on Lawrence Road off Frederica Road North. You can reach the site of Lawrence Plantation by car, but Cannon's Point is closed to the public. Taylor's Fish Camp is open daily except Thursdays.

B. Little St. Simons Island

The last of the family-owned barrier islands, Little St. Simons is a coastal paradise for bird watchers and nature enthusiasts. This 10,000-acre island once was part of Pierce Butler's Altamaha River rice-growing plantations and was a favorite all-day trip by barge for Fanny Kemble Butler. Lodging is available by private arrangement, and the island can be reached by a twenty-minute boat ride from the north end of St. Simons Island. Reservations must be made in advance, as there is no regularly scheduled ferry.

C. Sea Island (Long Island)

Called Long Island during plantation days, Sea Island was established in 1927 by Howard E. Coffin as a resort/residential community. Known as Fifth Creek Island, Isle of Palms, and Glynn Isle in former days, this home of the Cloister Hotel was part of Cannon's Point land. Privately managed by the Sea Island Company, the island hosts residents and guests at the Cloister, who may enjoy the island's beaches and beauty. This spot is considered one of the South's most popular honeymoon destinations.

D. Jekyll Island

Jekyll (called *Jakyl* by coastal islanders) probably got its name as a derivative of "Jacque's Island" (often called Jakes Isle), the pirate's station that operated there in the 1600s. In Oglethorpe's day, Jekyll Island was a military reserve under Captain Horton. Ownership after 1765 was: Clement Martin (1766); Richard Leake (1784), the prominent planter whose daughter married Thomas Spalding; Frenchman

Christopher Poulain duBignon (1790s), a former landowner of Sapelo Island (it was here among luxuries imported from France that Anna Matilda Page of Retreat Plantation took French lessons from Col. Henri duBignon's wife); a group of millionaires including the Rockefellers, Morgans, and Pulitzers (1886), who purchased it as a winter playground for their "Jekyll Island Club"; and, lastly, the State of Georgia (1947). Jekyll Island is approximately 7 miles long and 1 1/2 miles wide. To reach the island, take U.S. Highway 17 from Brunswick to the Jekyll Island Causeway.

13. Convention Center

Located on the beach, the center houses meeting rooms, an auditorium, and a fully equipped fitness center. The newly completed beach deck provides space for festivals and outdoor concerts and events.

14. duBignon House Ruins

These small ruins are located at Riverview and Major Horton drives. This site, which was home to five generations of duBignons, also contains the duBignon burial grounds.

15. Jekyll Island Museum

The largest restoration project in the southeast, the 240-acre Jekyll Island Club Historic District contains more than twenty-five buildings, many open for touring. It was registered as a National Historic Landmark District in 1978.

16. Horton House Ruins

Built in 1746, this house replaced the one burned by retreating Spaniards in 1742. This site is marked with a bronze plaque erected by descendants of William Horton, who was Jekyll's first English resident.

17. Millionaires Golf Course

Three 18-hole courses are included in this popular golf complex. The Oceanside Nine is the original course played by the millionaire members of the Jekyll Island Club.

Other interesting Georgia areas associated with the St. Simons and Georgia trilogies are included here in alphabetical order.

E. Blackbeard Island

Named for its reputation as an ideal hideaway for pirates, Blackbeard Island is east of Sapelo Island. In 1784, Don Juan McQueen bought Blackbeard along with Sapelo and several other sea islands. He sold them in 1789 to a Frenchman, François-Marie Loys Dumoussay de la Vauve, who defaulted on payments. An undeveloped barrier island, Blackbeard has been government owned since it was bought at public auction in 1800 by the U.S. Navy for the abundance of live oak timber that could be used in shipbuilding. From 1830 to 1900, Blackbeard was the site of a quarantine station for yellow fever. In 1940 it was designated as Blackbeard Island National Wildlife Refuge.

F. Blackshear

A small, inland town near the Satilla River on Highway 82 northeast of Waycross. Horace Gould used this location as a refuge for some of his family during the Civil War.

G. Blythe Island

Across the Marshes of Glynn on the eastern side of exits 7 and 7A of I-95, Blythe Island is between the Turtle and South Brunswick rivers. These tidewater estuaries empty into St. Simons Sound. Horace Bunch Gould worked here as an overseer for the absent owners.

H. Brunswick ❖ Brunswick Harbor

Brunswick is situated on the mainland across from St. Simons in Glynn County. Originally called Plug Point, the city was built on Capt. Mark Carr's colonial plantation (named Plug Point for the huge tobacco crop grown there). The Oglethorpe-style city plan (1771) called for a grid pattern of broad streets and parks. Original street names have been retained, and more than thirty-five significant sites have been preserved and identified. John Wylly was shot and killed here by Dr. Thomas Hazzard in December 1838 at the Oglethorpe House (no longer standing). The causeway to the

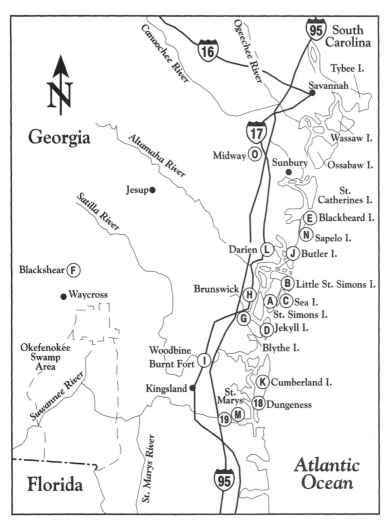

Map 5. Southeast Georgia–Points of Interest

E. Blackbeard Island
F. Blackshear
G. Blythe Island
H. Brunswick * Brunswick Harbor
I. Burnt Fort * Woodbine
J. Butler Island
K. Cumberland Island
   18. Dungeness

L. Darien
M. St. Marys
   19. Mills Ferry (Cabbage Creek)
N. Sapelo Island
   20. South-End House
O. Sunbury Historic Site *
   Midway Church

Golden Isles is accessible only from Brunswick.

In 1789 Brunswick was made a port of entry. In December 1861 federal gunboats blockaded the coast, and when Confederates guarding Brunswick were ordered to evacuate in February 1862, the wharf and railroad were destroyed. Federal occupation began on March 10, 1862.

I. Burnt Fort ❖ Woodbine

Burnt Fort Station was built in 1793 for the protection of Camden County (c. 1777) against raids by Creek Indians. In 1888, Anson Dodge established a mission here on the Satilla River near the town of Woodbine in Camden County. The present county courthouse was erected in 1928.

J. Butler Island

Pierce Butler, who introduced rice culture into Georgia in the late eighteenth century, owned this island south of Darien. The system of dikes and canals for the cultivation of rice is still in evidence here where he established a large rice plantation. Created by engineers from Holland, recently it has been used as a model for similar operations. Today the island is a part of the Altamaha River Waterfowl Area with the state headquarters for the area located on Butler Island. Persons interested in historical information and guided tours can find assistance at nearby Hofwyl-Broadfield Plantation and Fort King George.

K. Cumberland Island

This island was officially designated in 1972 as the Cumberland Island National Seashore, protected by the National Park Service. Sixteen miles long, it is the largest and southernmost of Georgia's barrier islands. A limited access of three hundred visitors a day makes for a peaceful and serene visit. Access is by ferry, and the landing is Dungeness Dock and Visitors Center at the northern tip of the island. Reservations and arrangements can be made at the visitors' center in St. Marys, which is the point of origin for the ferryboat.

18. Dungeness

Dungeness was designed as a grand mansion by Revolutionary

War hero Gen. Nathanael Greene, but his untimely death caused a ten-year delay in construction of the house. In 1796 the general's widow, Catherine Littlefield Greene, married Phineas Miller, a prominent politician. Building began on the enormous, four-story residence. The home became filled with people not only due to the marriage of the two Greene daughters (Martha Washington Greene to John Clark Nightingale; Louisa Catherine Greene to James Shaw), but because this massive tabby home was the center of entertaining along the coast.

One of the holiday house parties at Dungeness was interrupted by siege during the War of 1812. It was there that British Royal Marine lieutenant John Fraser met John Couper's daughter Anne. She and her best friend, Anna Matilda Page, were among the guests held captive at Dungeness by the British military when they invaded Cumberland Island. In the *Georgia Trilogy*, Eugenia Price based *Bright Captivity* and *Where Shadows Go* on the unalterable love Anne and John Fraser discovered and shared through a lifetime.

Dungeness and Cumberland Island play other roles in the Price novels, but the story of the Fraser couple's "captivity" of one another is the most important. Dungeness was inherited by Louisa Shaw—her sister Martha Nightingale and niece Louisa were rescued from drowning by James Hamilton Couper when the *Pulaski* sank in 1838 (in *Where Shadows Go*). Dungeness was rebuilt after being desecrated during Reconstruction days and then deserted until 1882. It was then that Thomas Carnegie built his Dungeness on the same foundation as the first. For almost a century, this mansion was bright with the social activities of America's wealthy elite. The house burned in 1959, leaving a haunting shell of past grandeur. In 1972 Cumberland Island became a National Seashore Park.

L. Darien

Located on the Darien River at the north branch of the Altamaha River, near the ruins of Fort King George (1721), Darien was established by Scottish Highlanders in 1736. Called New Inverness for a short time, Darien, the second oldest town in Georgia, had the first Presbyterian church in the colony. Its road to Savannah was the first highway built in the state.

By 1818, Darien was one of the great ports along the Atlantic coast. A lumbering, banking, and learning center for the nearby wealthy rice and cotton plantations, Darien had schools, hotels, churches, and its own hospital. Dr. William Fraser served that hospital and also became mayor of Darien before his death. Fraser and his wife (Frances Wylly of the Village Plantation, St. Simons Island) figured heavily in the *Georgia Trilogy*. Other references to Darien appear in the Price novels. In 1828, an exclusive organization of native Scots, the St. Andrews Society, was formed in Darien. John (Jock) Couper of Cannon's Point was its first president. Darien, whose history is spicy with sea captains, timber barons, and fisherman's tales, was burned during the Civil War in 1863. It is north of Brunswick on U.S. Highway 17 close to I-95.

M. St. Marys

This river town across the sound from Cumberland Island stands on a bluff and was once the site of a Timucuan Indian village. After Florida was given to England in 1763, large grants on the St. Marys River (the old Pagan Plantation) were made to South Carolina planters, among them Charles and Jermyn Wright, brothers of Sir James Wright, Georgia's last royal governor. Fort Tonyn was built near there at the start of the Revolution. It was named for British East Florida's Governor Tonyn. At one point called Buttermilk Bluff, St. Marys was built as a port town. Indian uprisings continually plagued St. Marys until Florida was ceded to the United States in 1819. Price mentions St. Marys throughout her novels, and it is included in this section because of its geographical placement. In *Margaret's Story* the Flemings' son George was installed as pastor of the First Presbyterian Church of St. Marys in 1857.

19. Mills Ferry (Cabbage Creek)

Site of Don Juan McQueen's Los Molinos tract. James Gould worked for McQueen as overseer of the saw mills (1797–1807).

N. Sapelo Island

Called Zapala by the Spaniards, this Georgia barrier island

appears to be connected to Blackbeard Island to the east but is separated by a web of inlets and tiny creeks. John McQueen owned both islands from 1784 to 1789. A group of French planters bought portions of the island and developed the north end around 1800. The Marquis de Montalet's home, Le Chatelet, was the domain of chef Cupidon. This chef trained Sans Foix, the culinary genius of John Couper's plantation, Cannon's Point on St. Simons Island.

20. South-End House

About the same time the north end of Sapelo Island was being developed, Thomas Spalding developed his plantation and mansion, South-End House. Spalding's slave Ben-Ali, the Mohammedan, was credited with helping win the War of 1812 by commanding the defense of Sapelo against the British. Spalding became known as the "Laird of Sapelo." In 1925, Howard Coffin rebuilt the South-End House, bringing renewed prominence to Sapelo as a retreat for dignitaries. Presidents Hoover and Coolidge were among those who visited. The property was purchased in 1933 by Richard J. Reynolds of North Carolina and further developed as a village complex. By 1976 the State of Georgia had acquired the entire island, with South-End House serving as headquarters for Marine Institute guided tours and environmental seminars. Georgia governors use the mansion for entertaining, and President Jimmy Carter's family vacationed there occasionally during his term in office.

O. Sunbury Historic Site ❖ Midway Church

The site of the "dead" town of Sunbury (seven miles east of I-95) and the New England–styled Midway Church and adjacent museum (on U.S. Highway 17) are located between Darien and Savannah. Colonial and Revolutionary Georgia history buffs will want to include each of these sites as they travel into Eugenia Price's South. It was here that Price's characters Rebecca Maxwell and John Couper met and married before settling at Cannon's Point Plantation. James Hamilton Couper, their first child, was born in Sunbury.

Map 6. Part 2–Florida Trilogy

PART 2

Florida Trilogy

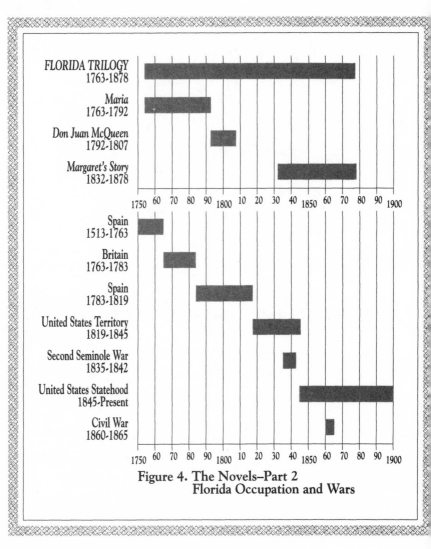

Figure 4. The Novels–Part 2
Florida Occupation and Wars

CHAPTER 4

The Novels

MARIA
DON JUAN MCQUEEN
MARGARET'S STORY

Three Eugenia Price novels followed the *St. Simons Trilogy*. They are collectively known as the *Florida Trilogy* and explore the areas surrounding the cities of Jacksonville and St. Augustine in the years 1763–1878. Price offers an insider's view of life in northeast Florida during the eighteenth and nineteenth centuries through the main characters whose names grace the titles: Mary Evans Fenwick in *Maria*; John McQueen in *Don Juan McQueen*; and Margaret Seton Fleming in *Margaret's Story*.

Don Juan McQueen* was written first (1974), although its chronological place in the trilogy is in the center. This well-liked, flamboyant character had made an introductory appearance in *Lighthouse*, when he gave James Gould the opportunity to manage the Mills Ferry tract on the St. Marys River at the Georgia/Florida border. Here again is evidence of Eugenia Price's technique—connecting the stories in the novels—that holds such fascination for us. The novels intermingle, the characters weaving in and out of Price's fictionalized, fact-based historical accounts of America's earliest days.

Don Juan is John McQueen's Spanish name—the one he embraced as he took on his new identity in the Florida territory under Spanish control. John McQueen could not return to Georgia because of his debts, and his family remained in Savannah struggling with his absence, never quite able to join him—physically, emotionally, or spiritually. This situation moves the plot forward with poignancy and, at the same time, opens the way for Price to rejoin McQueen's descendants in the Savannah Quartet (*see* Part 3).

For *Maria*, the novel about Mary Evans of Charles Town, South Carolina, Price takes a close look at the life of an enterprising woman who eventually married three times. Mary was allowed to accompany her first husband, British soldier David Fenwick, when his regiment fought the Spanish in Cuba. Then Spain agreed to give England all of Florida in exchange for the city of Havana. All British troops were ordered to remove from Cuba, thus forcing the couple to relocate to St. Augustine.

Once in St. Augustine, Mary Evans Fenwick (who became known as Maria) was able to use her skills as a midwife to provide additional income in the strange, new surroundings and to negotiate suitable living quarters for herself and her husband. Maria developed and enhanced her position with St. Augustine's influential citizenry during British occupation, so that twenty years later the return of Spanish domination in East Florida became for her an entrepreneurial opportunity rather than a threat.

Maria (published in 1977) goes back in time to pre-Revolution days in St. Augustine. England dominated the Florida province for twenty years of this story until the Spanish regained control after the Treaty of Paris ended the American Revolution. *Maria* therefore is best read first, as it sets the stage for *Don Juan McQueen*. In fact, true to her style, Price includes McQueen in the closing chapters of *Maria*.

McQueen, a "well-to-do Georgian," came, like many others, as a diplomatic visitor to observe the potential of tax-free land grants being offered by the rulers in Spanish-occupied Florida. McQueen had an interest in avoiding total ruin and possible imprisonment over tax debts. Florida would improve his income ability and bolster his dwindling personal holdings.

The Spanish Crown through the colonial period in Florida belonged to Charles III followed by Charles IV. Charles III (king of Spain), known while a young man as Don Carlos of Bourbon, was Charles IV (king of Naples) from 1734 to 1759. In 1759 he abdicated to become Charles III. When he died in 1788, Charles IV assumed the throne. His secret treaty with Napoleon of France in 1807 and the ensuing French invasion of Spain led to his abdication in 1808. It was Charles IV who empowered East Florida governor Enrique White to bestow an official title on Don Juan McQueen. Don Juan not only was a captain of the military for Spain but also judge of the Banks of the St. Marys and the St. Johns rivers and authorized to settle property disputes.

The final book in the *Florida Trilogy*, *Margaret's Story*, begins in 1832, eleven years after Florida was ceded to the United States. The steady influx of settlers into the new territory had caused increased tension with the native Indians—a prelude to the Seminole War (1835–41). Margaret Seton, daughter of Loyalists who had settled in British-held Florida in 1776, became the second wife of Lewis Fleming of Hibernia Plantation.

Located south of Jacksonville on the west shores of the St. Johns River, the 1000-acre Hibernia property, known as Fleming's Island, was granted to Lewis's father, George, who had emigrated to America from Ireland in 1780. George Fleming is mentioned in *Don Juan McQueen* as one of the settlers loyal to the Spanish.

As *Margaret's Story* begins, George Fleming has been dead nearly twelve years and Lewis is a newly widowed father of three. Margaret, at nineteen, knows she desperately loves the grief-stricken Lewis and that she must wait for him. While Lewis is away fighting Indians, Margaret endears herself to his children, particularly after the Seminoles burned Hibernia.

Margaret's Story relates Margaret Seton Fleming's unswerving love for Lewis, their marriage and rebuilding of Hibernia, the seven children she bore him, the hospitality she extended by opening

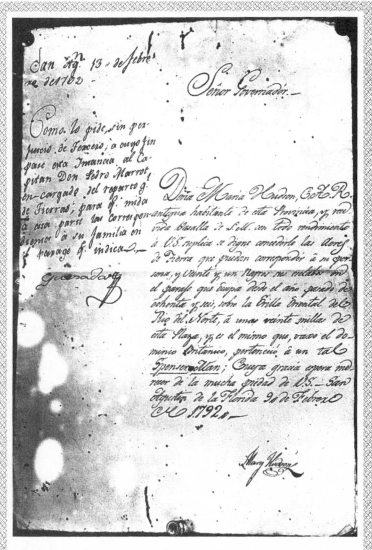

St. Augustine,
February 13, 1792

As she asks without injury to a third party, to which end let this communication go to Captain Don Pedro Marrot, in charge of general land distribution, so that he may measure those corresponding to the family of this party at the site indicated.

Quesada

Lord Governor

Doña Maria Hudson, Roman Catholic, long time resident of this Province and regarded as a subject of His Majesty, petitions your lordship, with all submission to be pleased to grant her those acres of land which might belong to her, and twenty one negroes, her slaves, at the site which she resides since the past year of 1786, on the eastern shore of the North River, about twenty miles from this City, which is the same that belonged to a Spenser Man during the British dominion, which grace she hopes she deserves from the utmost compassion of your lordship. St. Augustine, East Florida, February 9, 1792.

Mary Hudson

Petition (1792) by Mary Hudson and confirmation from Governor Quesada of land ownership on North River

Hibernia as a hotel, and finally the tragic effect of the Civil War on their family. Margaret's faith permeated their lives and is symbolized to this day by the chapel she built at Hibernia.

With all the vivid detail that illuminated the St. Simons Island saga, Eugenia Price has brought the complicated history of northeast Florida into focus through the lives of Maria, Don Juan, and Margaret. In this trilogy, Price skillfully continues to address human problems of that period: colony vs. crown; state vs. nation; Protestant vs. Catholic; planter vs. slave; landowner vs. squatter; native vs. settler. She blends a sense of home and place into the most difficult, lonely, or barren relationships so as to strengthen the resolve of her characters and the impact of the peace they find through their faith.

In Chapter 5 we will take a chronological look at the people and places covered by the *Florida Trilogy*: the Spanish colonial period; the twenty-year domination by the British; the return to Spanish control until statehood was achieved; and the eventual struggle between the Union and the Confederacy for the state of Florida.

The lives of the main characters in the *Florida Trilogy* and the history of the era are emphasized differently from those in Part 1 because of the geography and nature of the Florida territory. St. Simons Island was a community of planters and plantations. Northeast Florida was an ever-changing kaleidoscope of empires fighting for control.

Chapter 5 includes Charles Town, South Carolina, as background because of its importance to the English Crown and because Maria and Don Juan were reared there. Savannah, Georgia, will be covered in Part 3, which deals with the *Savannah Quartet* novels.

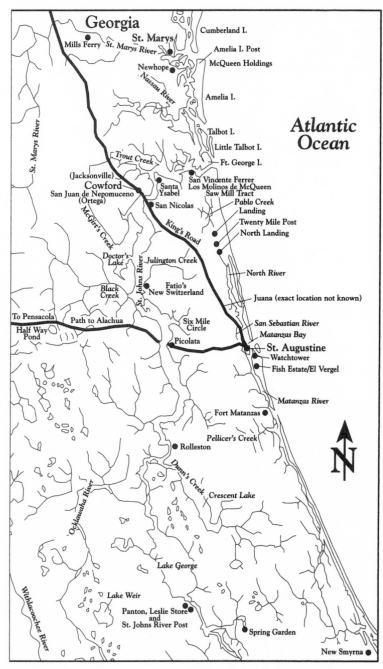

Map 7. Spanish East Florida (circa 1800)
From *Don Juan McQueen*, 1974

People and Places

Colonial Days

Beginning in 1565, when Don Pedro Menendez de Aviles founded St. Augustine, the Spanish Colonial Period in Florida lasted about two hundred years. It seemed that Spain had ambitions that reached beyond Florida. Strongly coveting the British colonies to the north, Spain sent an expedition from St. Augustine in 1742 to begin the conquest of those lands. The Spanish forces suffered a humiliating defeat at the hands of British general James Oglethorpe in the Battle of Bloody Marsh on St. Simons Island. A fairly brief engagement, this battle determined the character of the North American continent; it was to be predominantly English, not Spanish, from that point on. But the fight for Florida would not end that quickly.

The Peace of Paris in 1763 completely altered European colonial holdings in the New World. France ceded Louisiana to Spain's King Charles III and found itself without possessions in North America. England gained Canada and the upper Mississippi valley. Spain gave up its longstanding colony of Florida to England for the return of Havana, which the English had captured during the Seven Years War.

So it was that in 1763, King George III of England divided the former Spanish province into two separate colonies: West Florida, at Pensacola; and East Florida, at St. Augustine. The residents of St. Augustine had to leave their cherished homes and move to Cuba under a Spanish resettlement program.

The King of Spain appointed Don Juan Joseph Elixio de la Puente as royal auditor. He was to direct the transfer to Cuba, dispose of royal property in the city, and help Spanish Floridians sell their private property to the incoming British occupants.

It is here, in British East Florida, that Eugenia Price begins her story of Mary Evans Fenwick (Maria). Maria lived through both the British and the Spanish occupations of the frontier town of St. Augustine. Gen. Jeffrey Amherst was commander-in-chief of all British forces on the North American continent (c. 1763). In 1764 James Box of Savannah was appointed attorney general for St. Augustine. Dr. Robert Catherwood was one of the citizens of Charles Town who decided to live in St. Augustine since the city belonged to the British Crown. Dr. Catherwood, who knew Maria's father, Richard Evans, in Charles Town, would be a welcome sight for Maria and others so far from home.

Castillo de San Marcos

The history of the fort at St. Augustine creates a background setting for the *Florida Trilogy.* Constructed of natural shellstone (coquina), Castillo de San Marcos guarded a vital shipping lane that was the scene of constant power struggles among Spain, France, and England.

Early wooden forts were inadequate protection for the port city of St. Augustine. Spanish engineers worked with construction crews from 1672 until Castillo was completed in 1695. Through an eight-week siege in 1702 and one that lasted six weeks in 1740, the fort held strong. Spain gave all of Florida to Britain in 1762 so that Havana would be returned. Britain occupied the fort and St. Augustine from 1763 to 1784, but in 1783 the English gave Florida back to Spain.

Castillo de San Marcos, St. Augustine, Florida. (Courtesy of the St. Augustine Historical Society)

Thousands of Tories fled to British St. Augustine during the American Revolution. In 1780 prominent South Carolinians (labeled as American rebels) were brought by ship to Castillo de San Marcos (renamed Fort St. Mark by the British) and imprisoned. Spain held San Marcos from 1784 until 1821, when Florida became a U.S. territory and the name was changed to Fort Marion. Later the Confederacy controlled the fort for about a year during 1861–62.

Maria

Mary Evans was the daughter of Susan and Richard Evans of Charles Town, South Carolina. More than thirty years of her life were spent in Charles Town where she was born. That city and its citizens weave in and out of the *Florida Trilogy* as the empires of Europe fight for control of the American colonies and then as the Civil War breaks out.

Charleston, South Carolina

Founded in 1670 as Charles Town in honor of Charles II, king of England, this city was situated on the Atlantic coast at the confluence of the Cooper and Ashley rivers. In 1680 a band of Huguenots joined the community, and in 1755 about two thousand Acadian refugees arrived. The charter in 1783 changed the name to Charleston. This city was capital of South Carolina until 1789, when the capital was transferred to Columbia.

The port of Charleston was highly influential when rumblings of the Revolution began. By 1780 the British had captured the city and imprisoned its most prominent citizens on the ship *Jersey*, removing them to the San Marcos dungeon in St. Augustine, where they were held for a year. In 1861 Confederates fired the first shot of the Civil War at the union-occupied Fort Sumter in mid-harbor at Charleston. Within thirty-eight hours the fort was surrendered and remained in Confederate control until February 1865.

When England invaded Cuba in 1762, Mary Evans was allowed to leave Charles Town and go with her first husband, British soldier David Fenwick. Mary's best friend, Ann, married to British private James Cameron, also accompanied her husband to war.

Abruptly in July 1763, when Spain returned Florida to England, the British military and dependents were sent to occupy St. Augustine. Ann Cameron's ease with gossip helped Mary stay informed in that strange old city. In June 1769, Mary Fenwick was the midwife in attendance at the birth of the Cameron's daughter Nancy.

By 1780, James Cameron had joined Browne's Rangers to fight in the Revolution against the rebelling colonists. Thomas Browne was a refugee, a backcountry Carolinian who had been tarred, feathered, and partially scalped in Augusta, Georgia, for supporting the Crown. Browne's East Florida Rangers, along with their Indian allies, were instrumental in protecting St. Augustine from American forces during the Revolution (1776). When Cameron's death was reported to Ann and their daughter Nancy, the 1783 Treaty of Paris ending the Revolution had already been signed.

Mary became known as Maria to the Spanish citizens of St. Augustine. Maria's services as a nurse and midwife were of great value to her as a source of income and later as a solace when her husband, David Fenwick, died.

The first prestigious friend Maria made in St. Augustine was Jesse Fish, from whom she rented the Gonzáles house on St. Francis Street. Fish told Maria to see Don Luciano de Herrera about buying horses. Herrera was described to Maria by British captain Hedges as "a Spaniard of the Spaniards." Learning more about Fish and Herrera is important to our sojourn through northeast Florida.

Jesse Fish

Jesse Fish lived in St. Augustine under both Spanish and British rule. Fish was assumed to be rich from unscrupulous business schemes, land swindles in St. Augustine, and the exportation of Florida oranges. He is also known as the "Savior of St. Augustine," since he apparently saved the city from starvation in 1762–63.

Born in 1724 or 1726 in New York, Fish was sent to Florida in 1736 to learn about Spanish commerce for the William Walton Company of New York. He was placed with the Herrera family. By the age of fourteen, Fish became the knowledgeable link the Walton shipping firm needed. Later Fish acted as a sales agent, residing as a Protestant businessman in Catholic St. Augustine.

In 1762, Fish and some friends smuggled enough food into St. Augustine from South Carolina to save the old settlement from starvation. Since Spain and England were still at war, such trade could have been considered an act of treason. When 3,726 people departed from St. Augustine, according to the Treaty of Paris, the Spanish Floridians were permitted to sell their property to English subjects within an eighteen-month period. In July 1764, unable to find buyers, the Spaniards transferred about two hundred pieces of property, in and around St. Augustine, to Fish. Only forty-five days remained of the eighteen-month selling period when the transfer took place.

For Fish, the land deal with the Spaniards once again put him in a dangerous situation. English colonists like John Ainslie, Henry Laurens, John Holmes, James Moultrie, and his brother, Dr. John Moultrie, had indicated a desire to own land in Florida but had shown typical British restraint in choosing any property in St. Augustine proper. Fish also purchased property of his own, including Santa Anastasia Island, located across the harbor from St. Augustine. He built his home, El Vergel, on this island, which covered ten thousand acres along twelve miles of the Atlantic coast. El Vergel's flower gardens and orange groves flourished for many years, and the home became a well-known center for oranges by 1780.

Home of Jesse Fish, El Vergel on Anastasia (Santa Anastasia) Island, Florida. (Courtesy of the St. Augustine Historical Society)

Fish should have made a fortune from the sale and use of the Spanish property, but he did not keep necessary accounts of his business activities. His lifelong friend, Luciana de Herrera, prepared a record of some of his real estate transactions, and according to that work, Jesse Fish disposed of most of the property at a profit. Despite his high realty charges, sometimes as much as 30 percent of the sales proceeds, Fish owed "many thousands of pesos" to the Waltons, his former employer's family, and the previous property owners of St. Augustine.

During the last months of his life, Fish complained of limited funds and indebtedness. He retired to El Vergel in 1770 and remained a recluse for the rest of the British period to escape his personal problems. Fish gave the Spanish government all of his remaining holdings, except his home, to meet his debts to the former owners of St. Augustine property. Within a year Jesse Fish died and was buried at El Vergel.

Don Luciano de Herrera

Don Luciano de Herrera served as a spy for the Spanish during the American Revolution. From his home in British-controlled St. Augustine, he provided information for officials in Havana and Spain. Born in St. Augustine in 1736, he was the eldest son of Sebastián Mendez de Herrera, who had come to Florida from Spain. His mother was Doña Antonia, whose family had been in St. Augustine for more than three generations. Don Sebastián was prosperous and had commercial connections all along the Atlantic coast and throughout the Caribbean. For this reason in the 1730s the Walton trading firm of New York sent young Jesse Fish to live in the Herrera home. There Fish learned about Spanish commerce and formed a lifelong friendship with Luciano Herrera.

Herrera joined the militia as a youth. When the British occupied St. Augustine, Spanish royal auditor Puente left Herrera and seven other loyal subjects to oversee the disposal of property. Herrera called on his longtime friend Jesse Fish to help with the sale of real estate.

When the Spanish decided to monitor British activities in East Florida, Herrera operated a network of spies. The influential Puente's younger brother, Joseph Elixio de la Puente, arrived in St. Augustine in 1778 to work as an agent with Herrera.

Capt. Josef Chapúz was in command of a fleet of small fishing vessels that sailed between Havana and St. Augustine in the 1770s. Intelligence messages were sometimes concealed in letters by priests to the Cuban bishop and smuggled back and forth by way of the boats. The Spanish bishop in Havana then would relay news to Spain of British activities in St. Augustine. Weather conditions often hampered the espionage activities for months at a time.

Another messenger who worked with Herrera was Father Pedro Camps, the Minorcan priest at Andrew Turnbull's New Smyrna agricultural colony seventy-five miles south of St. Augustine on Mosquito Inlet. Father Camps used the fishing boats to send frequent letters to the bishop of Cuba. Luciano de Herrera thus kept his Spanish contacts informed of activities in British-occupied East Florida and St. Augustine.

Herrera was commended by Don Diego Joseph Navarro, Spanish captain general of Cuba, as a valuable source of information during the Revolutionary War. Herrera worked during a period of several years with the younger Puente brother, providing dispatches that were a regular source of vital information about British activities. When the Spanish government returned to East Florida after the Revolution, Herrera was appointed overseer of public works. This reward came through Governor Vicente Manuel de Zéspedes in the summer of 1784.

Zéspedes relied upon Herrera as the commissary for Indian relations and as a liaison with the representatives of Panton, Leslie, and Company in dealing with supplies to the Indians. Within a few years Herrera's health failed and he died in 1788.

Maria is laden with historical characters such as Jesse Fish and Luciano Herrera, who are part of the factual background that gives authenticity to the novel. Another character Eugenia Price brings to

Statue placed in memory of Father Pedro Camps, spiritual leader of the Minorcan colony in St. Augustine, Florida. (Courtesy of Suzanne Comer Bell)

life from historical records is Maria's house servant, whom she acquired through connections with Jesse Fish after David Fenwick's death (c. 1764). Long Stem, a young Indian woman, had worked at Government House and soon became an essential part of Maria's life. Maria moved from the cottage on St. Francis Street to her home on Charlotte Street at the north end of town. As a young widow, Maria's goal was to achieve security by becoming an independently wealthy woman. Her first step was to buy a house on Marine Street and rent it out.

Sometime after David Fenwick's death, Maria married English captain Joseph Peavett. Although Peavett was a Roman Catholic, Maria did not convert to Catholicism during their marriage. Earlier, Peavett had been a sergeant in the British service who acted as paymaster for the troops in East Florida. As the Revolution accelerated, the population of St. Augustine had swelled to more than five times its previous level. Peavett expanded his business interests, accumulating more than two thousand acres and almost sixty slaves, in addition to a house and property in St. Augustine. He was elected to the General Assembly and became an officer in the militia with the title of captain.

After Peavett bought the house and property across from the barracks on St. Francis Street (the property now known as the Oldest House), he and Maria operated a combination food store, tavern, and boarding house for the troops. Maria helped to operate the inn and worked as a midwife, one of the few respectable occupations open to women at that time. Maria was well suited for the job; she had no children, was the proper age, and was able to hurry to a woman's bedside at a moment's notice.

Maria's years as the wife of a prominent citizen added to her own prestige as a midwife. Although childless, she had three godchildren in addition to the adoptive relationship she developed with sixteen-year-old John Edward (Juan Eduardo) Tate. Young Tate, despite being orphaned since he was eight, had stayed strong through a series of tragedies. He was like a son to Maria, faithfully remaining with her and helping her no matter what happened. The final departure of British soldiers from St. Augustine in 1785 was reminiscent of the time two decades before when Spanish citizens evacuated to Cuba and left a depressed market for houses along mostly empty streets.

During what would be known as the Second Spanish Period, the previous residents would return from Cuba to find some changes to their former dwellings and also to find a few old friends still there, such as Jesse Fish, Francisco Xavier Sanchez, and Manuel

Front view of St. Francis Street House owned by Maria Evans Fenwick Peavett Hudson. (Courtesy of the St. Augustine Historical Society)

Soláno. Some British subjects remained to keep their estates and to start a new life—among them, John Leslie, Francis Philip Fatio, and Maria and Joseph Peavett.

By then about six hundred Minorcans lived in St. Augustine and were a continuing part of the Spanish-Catholic influence on the town's traditions. The Minorcans were a diverse group of colonists from New Smyrna, Florida, who had come to the New World as indentured servants under Dr. Andrew Turnbull. Turnbull had established his indigo plantation in 1767, but the experiment failed and his workers rebelled against the slave-like conditions. Besides true Minorcans, the refugees were a mixture of Turks, Greeks, and Italians and readily melded into a Spanish-Catholic allegiance in St. Augustine.

Thus British East Florida became, once more, Spanish East Florida. Maria's life changed even more at the death of Joseph Peavett, in April 1786, at age fifty-two. Maria, who was fifty-six when Peavett died, was left a prosperous widow. By late November of that year she became a Catholic, possibly to satisfy Spanish requirements for citizenship or possibly to please John Hudson. Hudson was twenty-eight years old and an Irish Catholic who had moved to St. Augustine from Havana at the beginning of the Second Spanish Period. Hudson and Maria were married on November 28, 1786.

In the first two years of their marriage, John Hudson caused the couple to go deeply in debt. Creditors, who knew of Maria's capital resources, clamored for repayment. Hudson asked that their largest plantation (named New Waterford in honor of his birthplace in Ireland) be used to pay the outstanding debt. Forced into bankruptcy, the Hudsons agreed to sell some of their furniture and tools. Suddenly other creditors asked for payment of their bills. The situation escalated and multiple lawsuits were filed.

John Hudson's drinking and insolent disrespect of authority caused his downfall. He was arrested in August 1790 and put into stocks at the Guard House. When Maria tried to get him released, he was placed in a cell at the Castillo to await trial. Banished from St. Augustine by Spanish governor Juan Quesada, Hudson moved to New Waterford, where he died in June 1791.

Father Thomas Hassett, the parish priest, was with Maria at her own death on September 30, 1792, at age sixty-two. In her will she freed four slaves and left New Waterford to John Edward Tate. She stipulated that the other slaves be allowed to live at New Waterford and not be sold. The most current research shows that Maria probably was buried, as requested in her will, in the Parochial Church cemetery, now called Tolomato Cemetery. Joseph Peavett and John Edward Tate are buried there also.

Don Juan McQueen

As we have seen in *Maria*, Eugenia Price provided an accurate feel for the Spanish-occupied territory that attracted and held a variety of citizens. Of chief interest to her readers is John McQueen, the intriguing country gentleman from Georgia featured in *Don Juan McQueen*. In 1791, McQueen hastily left his family in Savannah and sought refuge in St. Augustine. It was the year before Maria's death.

Of all the Price novels to date, Don Juan's story stands out as the most involved historical account and is the favorite of many readers who enjoy detailed accounts of post-Revolution days in America.

John McQueen was born in Philadelphia on September 18, 1751, and grew up in Charles Town, South Carolina. He was named for his greatly respected father who served in the Commons House of Assembly. The elder McQueen owned a successful mercantile firm, John McQueen and Company. The business sold goods to the Provincial Assembly, which in turn traded with the Indians for land rights. The eminent merchant also was a planter, owned large tracts of South Carolina property, and maintained a low-country plantation on Horse Savannah Creek in St. Paul's Parish, South Carolina.

The senior John McQueen died when young John was eleven, and his mother took the children to England for schooling. The widowed Ann McQueen, who was the oldest daughter of William and Sarah Dalton (originally from Kilkenny, Ireland), died in Europe not many years after losing her husband. Young John and his surviving brother, Alexander, returned to South Carolina and finished their educations under the guardianship of Charles Town attorney James Parsons.

Alexander, called Aleck by the family, became a successful merchant like the elder McQueen, but John's interest was quite different. He was obsessed with owning land. By the time John McQueen was twenty-six, he owned 9,300 acres in South Carolina and held partnership in 5,000 acres of Georgia timberland.

In 1772, when he was twenty-one, John McQueen married nineteen-year-old Anne Smith, daughter of wealthy rice planter John Smith and his wife, the former Elizabeth Williamson. John Smith had emigrated, as a young man, from Scotland to Charles Town. McQueen and his father-in-law were active supporters of the colonial efforts against the British.

John McQueen became a captain in the navy of South Carolina in 1778. The responsibility of that commission and his display of allegiance to the colonies fostered the development of the warm friendships McQueen enjoyed with George Washington and the

Marquis de La Fayette. In fact, McQueen traveled to France on behalf of Washington and was entrusted with dispatches for La Fayette and for Benjamin Franklin. By 1780, when Charles Town fell into British control, McQueen was thought to have been among those held on a prison ship in the harbor until the prisoners were exchanged. For a time after that, McQueen settled in St. Paul's Parish, South Carolina. He became a planter, supplying labor, rice, corn, and lumber to the Continental Army.

John and Anne Smith McQueen had five children, four of whom survived to maturity. In order of their births they were: John (b. 1773); Eliza Anne (b. 1778); Alexander (d. 1789 at age eight); William (b. circa 1782); and Sarah Williamson (b. 1784).

By 1784, his insatiable desire for land caused McQueen to change states and move his family to a small Georgia plantation on Thunderbolt Bluff near Savannah. He called this home the Cottage. Property that previously had belonged to Tories was being held by the Commissioners of Confiscated Estates and could be bought cheaply. Soon he owned other Georgia property: half of St. Catherine's Island and all of Sapelo, Little Cabretto, and Blackbeard islands, as well as land for a sawmill on the Savannah River, below Augusta.

As a citizen of Georgia, John McQueen was elected to the House of Representatives from Glynn County in 1788 and from Liberty County in 1789 (also representing that county to the Constitutional Convention of 1789). He was captain of the militia in Chatham County in 1790, and by January 1791 he was justice of the Chatham Inferior Court.

All his sea islands were sold in 1789 to a Frenchman, François-Marie Loys Dumoussay de la Vauve, who defaulted on the payment. McQueen started to find problems at every turn. Judgments against him for failure to pay taxes were posted in three counties: Camden, Chatham, and Glynn. He had mortgaged the Cottage at Thunderbolt in 1788, as the sale of timber had not been sufficient to pay the property taxes. By 1791 a judgment against him caused his hurried departure from Georgia to St. Augustine. His wife Anne's father and brother interceded, bought the Cottage property at auction, and thereby assured John McQueen's family of a place to live.

Part of the attraction East Florida held for John McQueen was the ready availability of land. Too, becoming a loyal subject of the Spanish Crown was not difficult for him, nor did he hesitate to embrace the Catholic faith. Once these two requirements were satisfied, John McQueen became in every reality Don Juan McQueen.

Don Juan bought a house on St. George Street in St. Augustine. His lot was next to the gardens of Governor Quesada's mansion. The McQueen plantation at Ortega was named San Juan de Nepomuceno in honor of Quesada's patron saint. McQueen and Quesada became close friends to their mutual advantage.

Don Juan's naval experience earned him the command of a coastal expedition against William Augustus Bowles. Known as a pirate, Bowles was from Maryland and Don Juan McQueen spent time chasing but never apprehended him. Although Bowles was not an Indian, he attempted (into the 1790s) to become head of the Seminoles. He was closely associated with Britain and planned to establish a new nation—Muskogee. His plans failed, and in 1805 he died in a Spanish prison, but not without stirring up trouble in the Floridas with the Creek Indians.

The house built by Don Juan McQueen, now the Kingsley Plantation Historic Site, Fort George Island, Florida. (Courtesy of Suzanne Comer Bell)

For these services, the Spanish rewarded Don Juan with a valuable grant of land at the mouth of the St. Johns River–Fort George Island. He built a home at the north end of the island and established his sawmills nearby. This was the area known as Los Molinas de McQueen.

Quesada retired to Cuba but not before making other grants to Don Juan. The last of these was two thousand acres at Cape Florida. The Spanish Crown recognized McQueen's value and loyalty, thereby giving him military commands and authority that influenced other settlers to side with Quesada's Rural Militia.

Gen. Elijah Clark was a leader in the American Cavalry during the Revolution. In the Florida–Georgia border uprising (known as the East Florida Rebellion of 1795), General Clark recruited forces and promised them rich land when the Spanish were forced out of Florida. This was not to happen, although the unrest continued deeper into Spanish territory, almost reaching St. Augustine.

In 1794 Capt. Peter Carne was one of the East Florida settlers who remained loyal to Spain. After Rebels captured the Spanish outpost at Juana, nine miles north of St. Augustine, Carne reported the names of those involved to Governor Quesada, who called a council of war on July 4, 1795. In order to squelch the trouble, they sought Don Juan's advice. Spanish troops stopped the serious eruption of violence along the Florida–Georgia border in 1795 and recaptured Jacksonville and nearby Amelia Island within a short period. The Spanish troops arrested two of the most dangerous rebels, John McIntosh and Abner Hammond, and arranged to have them transported to prison in Havana aboard Capt. Miguel Costa's sloop *Maria*. Costa was to deliver his prisoners and give word of the uprising to Spanish officials in Cuba.

Don Juan McQueen was awarded several commissions by the grateful Spanish officials. In 1798 he was appointed "Captain of Militia and Commandant of the St. Johns and St. Marys Rivers." By 1801 Enrique White, who had been governor of West Florida in 1793–95, then of East Florida since 1796, named Don Juan "Judge of the River Banks."

McQueen's services in 1802 as lieutenant colonel were valuable in the interior struggle with the Indians. To the west and south of St. Augustine, Don Juan held the Creek Indians in check. The Oconee band of Creek Indians had migrated to that region of Florida from the Oconee River in central Georgia following the Yamassee War (1715). One group—the Alachua band—became the nucleus of the Seminole tribe (c. 1750). In McQueen's time people referred to the area west of St. Augustine simply as Alachua. The area sixty miles to the south was called the Mosquitoes. It was there Don Juan held forth until Creeks ratified a treaty with the Spanish.

During all this time Don Juan's wife Anne and their children lived at the Cottage in Georgia. Eugenia Price aptly develops McQueen's relationship with his family through letters and the rare and dangerous trips he makes into Georgia. Anne McQueen made one memorable visit to St. Augustine, in particular, at which time she confronted her long-held antipathy for her husband's Spanish way of life and his conversion to Catholicism. Anne McQueen desperately loved Don Juan but could not change her citizenship nor her religion. Concerns for her and the young children's safety and well-being were primary, yet at the same time she needed and longed to be with her husband.

Don Juan's fortunes rose and fell throughout his life. He, too, wished to be with his wife and family and struggled to resolve his obligations to them by making the best of his situation in Florida. Having property to bequeath to his heirs became an obsession. Two of McQueen's children become important to Eugenia Price's continuation of the McQueen story into the *Savannah Quartet*: John Jr. and Eliza Anne.

Sometime in 1795, Don Juan placed John Jr. with the trading firm of Panton, Leslie and Company in Pensacola, where William Panton was to train McQueen's elder son. About 1800, young John left the mercantile business and returned to Georgia to become a planter. He bought Causton's Bluff near Savannah in 1802, married his cousin on his mother's side, Margaret Cowper (1810), and was recognized for successfully introducing ribbon-type sugarcane into the United States. He died near Savannah in 1822 with no heirs.

McQueen's daughter Eliza Anne's visits to her father in St.

Augustine and their correspondence must have helped Don Juan in his loneliness for the family. In Eugenia Price's plot development, McQueen endorsed Eliza Anne's engagement to merchant Robert Mackay of Savannah. They would be married on January 30, 1800, at the Cottage.

Eugenia Price drew on Don Juan's actual letters for insight into his opinions and reactions. The summer before the wedding, after a visit from Robert Mackay, Don Juan wrote: "St. Augustine, 12th July 1799, My dear Eliza . . . I really my dear Girl in a few words must tell you that I highly approve of your choice. . . ." McQueen had known Robert Mackay's father in South Carolina before the Revolution and was pleased that his future son-in-law had risen so rapidly in the mercantile business.

Before 1800, Robert Mackay had been junior partner to William Mein. Their Savannah business firm of Mein and Mackay continued to prosper long after Mackay's marriage to Eliza Anne. (*See* Part 3 for more about Eliza Anne McQueen Mackay, the matriarch of the *Savannah Quartet*, and for those Savannah points of interest found in *Don Juan McQueen*.)

Don Juan McQueen's interaction at each level—political, social, commercial, spiritual—demonstrated the keen sensitivity and magnetism of his personality. He was a communicator whose letters show an ease with relationships and an eagerness for a peaceful life.

Eugenia Price allowed Don Juan's Florida friendships to be genuine and diverse as she knew them to be: he played checkers with John Leslie (the Scottish merchant in *Maria*) and with the Irish priest Father Miguel O'Reilly; he shared a unique place of favor with Spanish royal governor Quesada and his family; he took courage and blessing from the Franciscan Father Narcisco Font; he shared the need for steadfastness and comfort with his Minorcan neighbor Señora Ysabel Perpal; he received respect from the militia and enjoyed loyalty from his servants—the faithful slave Harry (who at age twelve had come with him from Georgia), the Minorcan houseboy Pedro, and the silent Black Katrina (abandoned by British owners with the return of Spanish rule).

Thriving on loyalty in his relationships, McQueen remained

faithful to his religious convictions, to his wife, and to his family throughout his remaining years. He was held in such high regard that at his death (October 11, 1807) Royal Governor Don Enrique White sent a dragoon from St. Augustine to bring Don Juan's body to the city for an ecclesiastical burial.

McQueen had died suddenly (apparently from typhus fever) forty-two miles away at Los Molinas de McQueen, his home on Fort George Island. Don Juan's faithful Harry, who was by that time twenty-nine years old, attended his master to the end, bathed and dressed him in his uniform, and at the doctor's orders helped to bury him. When Don Bartolomé de Castro arrived with the dragoon, he had Don Juan's body removed from the grave and readied for the long escorted trek back to St. Augustine. The burial description was signed by Father Miguel O'Reilly, the Vicar of St. Augustine, Don Juan's checkers partner, confidant, and priest. These last solemn acts of devotion by the Spanish governor and the Catholic priest gave credence and finality to the allegiances that made John McQueen truly Don Juan McQueen.

Margaret's Story

In developing a third novel for the *Florida Trilogy*, Eugenia Price brought together the threads of the British and Spanish periods in northeast Florida by giving us a love story. Margaret Seton and Lewis Fleming were of the first generation born to parents who settled in Florida before the territory belonged to the United States. Their saga includes the richness of British and Spanish influences, the trials of the Second Seminole War, the prosperity of statehood and the plantation era, and the devastation of the Civil War. The events that took place after we left Don Juan McQueen changed the Floridas forever.

The Second Spanish Period in Florida lasted some twelve years following the death of Don Juan McQueen in 1807. The first treaty in the United States' acquisition of Florida came in 1819. In St. Augustine the change of the flag and authority from Spanish to American took place in 1821. A new regime welcomed investors

from nearby states in hopes of bolstering St. Augustine's slow econ-
omy. Andrew Jackson was appointed governor of the Floridas to
handle the transfer from Spain to the United States. His offices were
in Pensacola.

At the beginning of *Margaret's Story* (1832), Florida had been in its
territorial phase for eleven years. A struggle between Pensacola
(West) and St. Augustine (East) for becoming the seat of government
was so heated that statehood would be delayed until 1845. The
influx of white settlers into the South had caused resentment and
tension among Florida's Seminole Indians for years. The advancing
white frontier that attracted entrepreneurs forced Indian tribes from
neighboring states into Florida. The Seminole situation exploded,
and the disputes over land escalated into the Second Seminole War
(1835–42).

In *Margaret's Story* Eugenia Price draws the readers into the life of
Florida native Margaret Seton, a young woman who at nineteen
years of age decided someday she would marry widower Lewis
Fleming of Hibernia. Margaret was the daughter of Charles and
Matilda Sibbald Seton of Fernandina on Amelia Island, Florida. She
had one sibling, a brother, George.

Margaret's father, Charles Seton, was the son of Loyalists from
the colony of New York who had sought refuge in British-held
Florida in 1776. The family had remained there and, like so many
others, started a new life. Seton's wife, Matilda, was the daughter of
Mr. and Mrs. Charles Sibbald. who lived at Panama Mills on the St.
Johns River five miles north of Jacksonville. Known as Cowford
until the 1820s, Jacksonville was chartered in 1832 and became a
thriving antebellum lumber port town. Charles Sibbald owned and
operated a giant steam sawmill at Panama Mills.

The dominant setting for *Margaret's Story* is Hibernia Plantation
on Fleming's Island, twenty miles south of Jacksonville along the
western banks of the St. Johns River. This great house and plantation was built on a 1,000-acre Spanish land grant by Lewis
Fleming's father, George, who came to America in 1785 from his
native Ireland. The Flemings named their plantation for their home-
land, as *Hibernia* is Latin for Ireland.

George Fleming married Sophia Philipina Fatio, one of seven Fatio daughters of Francis Philip Fatio, Sr., and his wife, Marie Madeline Crispel. Fatio had migrated to Florida in 1771. His family had a home on the bay in St. Augustine and three large plantations on the St. Johns River. Their country residence was the largest of these holdings—ten thousand acres across the river from Hibernia that Fatio named New Switzerland (Nueva Suiza) for the country of his youth. His wife died in 1810, followed by his death in 1811. They were buried at New Switzerland.

The first son born to George and Sophia Fatio Fleming was Lewis Michael. Although the Flemings lived in St. Augustine at the time of his birth, soon the family returned to Hibernia on Fleming's Island, where Lewis grew up. Lewis was close to his Fatio cousins across the St. Johns. His mother's brother, Francis Philip Fatio, Jr., had married Susan Hunter of Philadelphia in 1796. Miss Hunter had come to Florida hoping to be cured of pulmonary consumption. She had two daughters, Louisa and Eliza, before that disease took her life. Fatio's second wife, Mary Ledbetter, had five children before her death in 1828. Fatio, Jr., died in the spring of 1831.

In 1812 New Switzerland and Hibernia were raided and were the first houses burned by Seminole Indians. The Fatio family escaped to St. Marys, Georgia, and while the house at New Switzerland was being rebuilt, the Fatio family lived for a time at Fernandina on Amelia Island. During the Patriot rebellion, about that same time, American adventurers attempted to seize Spanish Florida's borderlands. Lewis Fleming's uncle, Francis Fatio, Jr., and Margaret's father, Charles Seton, fought together in a skirmish at Waterman's Bluff. Seton's leg was wounded.

As a very young child, Margaret Seton learned to love the Fatio family, who were living near her home at Fernandina. She knew all the brothers, sisters, and cousins; Louisa Fatio, eldest daughter of Francis Philip Fatio, Jr., became Margaret's best friend, despite the fact that Louisa was fifteen years older than Margaret. When the Fatio family moved back to New Switzerland, Margaret visited Louisa often.

In late December 1832, the Setons accompanied the Fatio family from New Switzerland to "cousin" Lewis Fleming's home at Hibernia across the St. Johns River for the funeral of his wife, Augustina Cortez Fleming. Louisa's first cousin Lewis and Augustina had been married for ten years; they had two sons, George and Louis Isadore (L. I.); a new baby girl was named Augustina (Tina) for her mother, who had died in childbirth.

Eugenia Price used that burial scene at Hibernia as a natural beginning for *Margaret's Story*. Conversation and comfort and tears flowed among the relatives and friends—Fatio, Fleming, Seton— each connected by blood or friendship. Margaret Seton confided in Louisa that she would some day marry Lewis Fleming. Margaret was struck by the despair she saw on Lewis's face as he stood with his two young sons at the graveside, an infant daughter in his arms. Margaret simply knew she loved Lewis, a love that would only deepen for him and Hibernia as time passed. Margaret returned to Fernandina with her parents, and, except for holidays at New Switzerland, she did not see Lewis.

In December 1835, Maj. Lewis Fleming was called into active duty with the U.S. Florida Regulars to fight the Seminoles. He reported to Jacksonville and then to St. Augustine, where he was to gather volunteers for the militia and ride south to Fort Drane. Lewis left the children with Cousin Louisa at New Switzerland. Louisa had others in her charge but was closest to her half-sister, Sophia, who also could assist in the care of the Fleming children. In just a few weeks, Margaret Seton would come for the holiday season and could help.

By December 14 news came that twenty-two houses in Alachua County had been burned to the ground. A Florida inland colony, situated in the center of the Alachua band of Seminole Indians, had been started there in late 1820. This settlement was named Micanopy for the head chief and was the first town established by whites that was not located near waterways.

Lewis's rank of major gave him the task of keeping peace among the volunteers and the Regulars as they traveled together to Fort Drane. Fort Drane was actually Auld Lang Syne, a plantation belonging to Gen. Duncan Lamont Clinch that was four miles square and planted in sugarcane. It was located about ten miles from Micanopy, east of the St. Johns River and south of St. Augustine. General Clinch named his plantation-turned-fort for its builder, Capt. Gustavus Drane. The sixty men Drane brought safely through the Seminole Nation had nicknamed it Fort Drane. The conditions were wretched, insect-ridden, and crude.

A few days after Christmas, the troops (seven hundred by then) were ordered by Gen. R. K. Call to advance to an area three miles from the Withlacoochee River where they would bivouac on the night of December 30. The volunteers had been told they could go back to their homes on January 1, 1836, so the attack was ordered. History records that this battle may have done more harm than good, but two facts were proven: (1) these hostilities did indeed constitute a war; and (2) the citizen soldiers believed their duty was to protect their own homes while the regular army would not move without proper orders—orders that could not reach them if they were cut off from their command.

Fighting Indians in an open area would have been possible, but when the soldiers attacked the Indians in the density near the Withlacoochee River, they melted from sight, leaving heavy casualties for the Florida troops. Lewis Fleming was among the wounded who were carried back to Fort Drane in what became more a hospital than a fort.

Young John Bemrose aided Dr. Weightman at Fort Drane and personally cared for Lewis Fleming after Fleming was wounded at Withlacoochee. Eugenia Price's prose reveals the compassion Bemrose showed for the men and the particular energy he put into Fleming's recovery. During the Second Seminole War (1835–42) Bemrose served in the U.S. Regular Army as a surgeon's steward. Young and British, he kept interesting notes about the mixture of nationalities fighting Seminoles together. Eugenia Price used these notes to recreate an accurate, vivid depiction of the people who lived during this frightening period.

While Price portrays the Seminole War and this part of *Margaret's Story* with careful authenticity, she found it useful to create a fictional character, Leroy Black, who rode as a citizen soldier with

Maj. Lewis Fleming. Black was the owner of a small forty-acre dirt farm on the outskirts of St. Augustine. He symbolized the volunteers who feared they would die and leave their families unprotected and without providers.

Price's characterization of the conflicts between Gen. R. K. Call and the other officers, particularly General Clinch, followed the historical record of Call's ambition and drive. Virginia native Gen. Richard Keith Call was appointed in early spring 1836 as territorial governor of Florida by his old friend, then President Andrew Jackson. Call, who grew up in Kentucky, volunteered to fight in the Creek War (1813) under Jackson's command with the Tennessee militia. Their friendship continued after the war, including a term in the eighteenth Congress. Because President Jackson had served as Florida's first territorial governor in 1821, he was well aware of the hostilities Call would face, and, unlike numerous others, he appreciated Call's ambition and drive for personal honor. These attributes, however, became a negative force in their friendship of twenty-three years, and Call was replaced in December 1836.

Price alternates scenes from Fort Drane to the Fatio family gathered at New Switzerland. Her description of their narrow escape from the Fatio plantation after seeing Hibernia in flames across the St. Johns adds suspense and momentum to the story. They waited at the Seton home on Amelia Island for Lewis Fleming to return. As Fleming hung precariously between life and death, John Bemrose's care saved him and even preserved Fleming's shattered leg.

Lewis did return, and he and Margaret were married and eventually had seven children: Charles Seton; Francis Philip (Frank, who became Florida's fifteenth governor); Frederic Alexander; William Henry; Matilda Caroline (Tissie); Margaret Seton (Maggie); and Isabel Frances (Belle).

Margaret's grandfather Charles Sibbald hired Lewis to manage his large lumber operation at Panama Mills. It was there in early 1839 that Seton was born; their second son, Frank, came in the fall of 1841. Today Panama Mills is a Jacksonville suburb called Panama Park.

The Flemings left the mills in November 1841 to make their

home at Hibernia. Lewis and Margaret shared the dream of rebuilding Hibernia, as well as one day building a chapel of their own. They would live in an old warehouse that had been remodeled for a dwelling until a new home could be built. The plantation house was finished around 1857 and operated as a Southern retreat for visitors from the North, just as Cousin Louisa had done with success in St. Augustine.

Louisa Fatio, who had seen New Switzerland burned by Indians for the second time in her life, had decided it would be the last time; she would not rebuild the Fatio plantation. She chose instead to lease a house in St. Augustine and open it to boarders. She first located near the bay, then on Charlotte Street close to the barracks, and finally in a large house on the corner of Hospital Street and Green Lane that she purchased in 1855.

Guests at Ximénez-Fatio boarding house run by Louisa Fatio. (Courtesy of the St. Augustine Historical Society)

Known today as the Ximénez-Fatio house, Louisa's home was built in 1797 by Andres Ximénez of Rondo, Spain. On the property was a coquina block house with tabby floors. There were two warehouses along the west lane and a separate coquina kitchen. The ground floor was used as a general store with living quarters above.

When U.S. authorities took over in St. Augustine in 1821, Margaret and Samuel Cook of Charleston had purchased the property from the heirs of Ximénez. After Samuel's death in 1826, Margaret Cook converted the buildings into an inn. It was managed by Elizabeth C. Whitehurst until her death in 1838. Sometime between 1830 and 1845, the inn underwent a major remodeling, either by Margaret Cook or another owner, Mrs. Sarah P. Anderson. The renovations allowed for a spacious boarding house that made use of the earlier structures.

Louisa Fatio operated a popular and fashionable inn for twenty years until her death in 1875. Her neighbors Sarah Anderson and Lizzie Smith (remembered as Mrs. Judge Smith, mother of Confederate general Edmund Kirby-Smith) add flavor to the plot of *Margaret's Story* during the period of the Civil War.

In January 1858, Lewis and Margaret welcomed their first visitors to the great house at Hibernia. Mr. and Mrs. Jerome Bonham, a Massachusetts couple, and their niece Miss Lucy Malloy were charmed by their host and hostess, the liveliness of so many children, the sumptuous, well-prepared meals, and the eager attentiveness of the servants.

From their approach, visitors admired the handsome mansion situated back from the St. Johns River. Leading from the wharf to the house was a double row of pink crepe myrtles; paths to the barns and to the quarters (for more than one hundred slaves) were planted in twin rows of water oaks. The house itself boasted seven tall chimneys of soft red brick rising above the three-story, white live-oak structure. Hand-hewn square pillars supported the roof, green shutters trimmed the windows, and gracious wide porches on two sides seemed to exude hospitality. In a few weeks fifteen guests were enjoying life at Hibernia.

Margaret's dream of building a chapel at Hibernia was not forgotten, only delayed. A devout Episcopalian, Margaret was ecstatic when in 1856 the Right Reverend Alonzo Potter (bishop of Pennsylvania) confirmed Lewis into the Episcopal church. Despite this happiness, Hibernia was not without a mixture of joy and sadness. News of their son George's death from a heart attack came on the same day as the letters that told them L. I. had been appointed Florida's state attorney and that Seton had been accepted at King's Mountain Military School in South Carolina.

The steamboat captain had brought the three letters along with one thin, graying passenger, George Causey. Causey was a lonely widower from Pennsylvania who had come to vacation at Hibernia. He was sixty-six years old and was on a pension from the ironworks where he had been a bookkeeper. Causey, who asked if he could stay at Hibernia past the season and find a way to earn his keep, was a strong addition to the Fleming family. Somehow he entered their lives just when he was the most needed.

Services were held for Lewis Fleming's oldest son, Rev. George Fleming of St. Marys, who was buried beside his mother, Augustina. Margaret and Lewis had seen sensitive, deep-thinking George through medical school and the upheaval of his marriage to Mary Bennett once he pursued ordination to the Presbyterian ministry.

This was a time that it probably seemed more important than ever for Margaret to build a chapel at Hibernia, although it would have been impossible for her to know the grief-filled days that were to come. By 1860 each of her four sons would fight for the Confederacy—Frank and Seton would volunteer immediately.

In 1862 word from Cousin Louisa was that Christobal Bravo, the Minorcan who was acting mayor of St. Augustine when Federal troops occupied the city, had raised a white flag at Fort Marion that could be seen by Union gunboats. War brought an end to Florida vacationers and ample supplies.

For those left isolated at Hibernia, the devastation would worsen. On August 3, 1862, Margaret sent word to Louisa that Lewis had died and requested that she try to bring an Episcopal minister for the services. Rev. John Cannings, a retired Episcopal rector living in

Saint Margaret's Episcopal Church

Hibernia, Florida

Drawing of Margaret's chapel and churchyard from bulletin of St. Margaret's Hibernia Episcopal Church, Green Cove Springs, Florida. (Drawing by Tamara Culbert)

St. Augustine, went by boat with Louisa Fatio to Hibernia to give Lewis Fleming a Christian burial. Cannings was from the North but chose to remain in St. Augustine for the war years. A Union pass gave the mourners forty-eight hours to have the funeral, comfort the family, and return.

Not long afterward, the other two boys left to join the war effort. Margaret and her three daughters, George Causey, and a few faithful slaves were alone at Hibernia in 1864 when Union brigadier general William Birney signed the order to evacuate all inhabitants except "old men and Negroes" from Fleming's Island.

Miraculously Margaret and her daughters traveled safely to Lake City, Florida, where they could be with L. I. and his wife, Mary Evelyn (L'Engle). Margaret worked tirelessly at the military hospital always hoping someone, somewhere would care as much for her sons. Word reached her there that Seton had been killed.

At the war's end in 1865, Frederic returned to Hibernia to supervise the repairing and rebuilding of their beloved home. Margaret was able to reopen Hibernia for boarders in the spring of 1866. Some six years later, she wrote Louisa that work on her chapel in the woods had begun. Her fund built slowly, as other expenditures came first; after all, there was a boardinghouse to run.

In 1875 Louisa died and was buried at New Switzerland with others of the Fatio family. Maggie Fleming died in 1877 from yellow fever while nursing her brother Frank and his family in Jacksonville. Margaret Seton Fleming's funeral was held on April 6, 1878, at her chapel in the woods, though work on it was not completed.

The chapel, consecrated in 1894 as St. Margaret's Episcopal Church, was named for an early Christian martyr. The Hibernia congregation uses Margaret Fleming's funeral as the chapel's anniversary since the first services were held on that date.

Eugenia Price expertly molds fact and fiction through her characters in the *Florida Trilogy*, giving her readers more than one hundred years of life in the northeast Florida wilderness and the emerging cities of what would become America's twenty-seventh state. A visit to the old city of St. Augustine is not just a look at one period covered by a single family but a stroll through several generations whom Price has brought to life in *Maria, Don Juan McQueen*, and *Margaret's Story*.

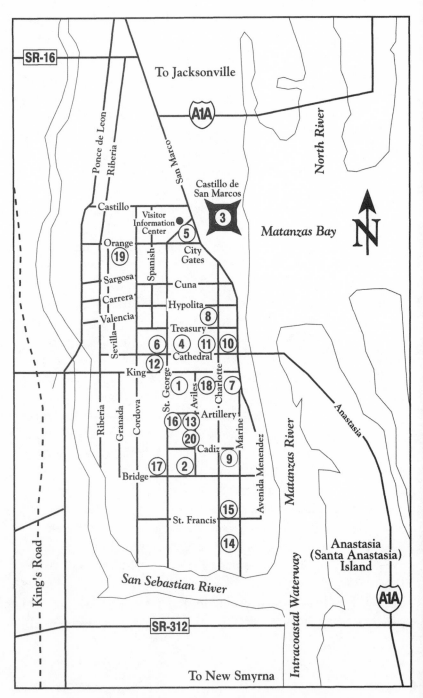

Map 8. St. Augustine, Florida–Points of Interest

CHAPTER 6

Points of Interest

ugenia Price used St. Augustine as the background for *Maria*, *Don Juan McQueen*, and portions of *Margaret's Story*. Many of the sites the Price characters knew can be seen today, some still as they saw them, some reconstructed, some vacant, and some now covered with later buildings. Price used very few purely fictional sites in the *Florida Trilogy*, so only the factual locations are covered in this chapter.

A. St. Augustine
  1. Bishop's Palace
  2. Casa O'Reilly
  3. Castillo de San Marcos National Monument
  4. Cathedral of St. Augustine
  5. City Gates
  6. DeBrahm House
  7. Fatio House
  8. Luciano de Herrera House
  9. Marine Street House
  10. Panton and Leslie Store
  11. Payne's Corner
  12. Plaza and Government House
  13. St. Augustine Public Library
  14. St. Francis Barracks
  15. St. Francis Street House (Oldest House)
  16. St. George Street House
  17. St. Peter's Church
  18. Spanish Hospital
  19. Tolomato Cemetery
  20. Ximénez-Fatio House

A. St. Augustine

1. Bishop's Palace

In 1766 Rev. John Forbes made repairs to the second floor of the old Spanish Bishop's Palace on the Square in St. Augustine so services could be held. This "Anglican Church" site is occupied today by Trinity Episcopal Church (c. 1825).

2. Casa O'Reilly

This house where Don Juan McQueen's checkers partner, Father Miguel O'Reilly, lived is now part of the Convent of the Sisters of St. Joseph. The house at 34 Aviles Street is closed to the public, but you can view the exterior.

3. Castillo de San Marcos National Monument

This is the oldest original building in the United States and was already more than one hundred years old when Maria stayed there her first night in St. Augustine. The history of the fort is covered in Chapter 5, as it was central to events in the *Florida Trilogy*.

4. Cathedral of St. Augustine

Parts of Don Juan McQueen's parish church were used in building the cathedral, located at Cathedral Place and St. George Street.

5. City Gates

Built in 1739, the gates are to the right as you leave Castillo de San Marcos. The gates provided the only access through defense lines on the north side of the city. From the Castillo, Maria walked through the gates and down St. George Street the first time she explored the town.

6. DeBrahm House

In *Maria*, Jesse Fish sold William DeBrahm, royal surveyor, "the fine house on St. George Street adjoining Government House Gardens." Today the southeast corner of the Barnett Bank parking lot occupies the DeBrahm site. Cathedral Place west of St. George Street replaces the gardens.

7. Fatio House

Records show that the elegant house Francis Philip Fatio, Sr., purchased on the bay and several other properties he owned were close to Charlotte and Marine streets at King Street. That portion of Marine Street would have bordered the bay in the 1700s.

8. The Luciano de Herrera House

Eugenia Price describes the home as "a six-roomed, two-storied coquina house, in need of a cleaning and a coat of paint inside and out, but the roof's in good repair, the windows all glazed. There is one fireplace in the parlor, and another can be opened in the bedroom above." The site at 58 Charlotte Street presently is occupied by a restoration of the house where Maria lived when she was a young widow and during the time she and her second husband remodeled their St. Francis Street house. It was constructed in 1967 by the Southern Bell Telephone Company for its office, now closed.

9. Marine Street House

When Maria sold David Fenwick's house, she bought property on Marine Street, which she rented. In reality, Maria kept a house on the west side of Marine Street following the forced sale of her other properties. In the inventory made after her death in 1792, it is described as a "house of tabby and wood with its partition, two-story and kitchen attached; a chimney in the parlor and another in the kitchen. . . ." Its exact location is not known today.

10. Panton and Leslie Store

The store may have been on the southwest corner of the bay front and Treasury Street. Today the approximate location is the entrance to the Atlantic Bank drive-in windows.

11. Payne's Corner

In the British period Robert Payne owned the property where

notices were posted at Charlotte Street on the north side of the Square. Near the site today is a bookstore.

12. Plaza and Government House
The center of St. Augustine for almost four hundred years, the Government House was where Maria's third husband was placed in stocks for abusing the Spanish governor's authority. The Government House, extensively remodeled over the years, occupies the site where Maria and Don Juan McQueen conducted their official business and attended plays and banquets.

13. St. Augustine Public Library (former site)
The former home of Confederate sympathizer Mrs. Judge Smith (Lizzie), neighbor of Margaret's friend, Louisa Fatio. Confederate general Edmund Kirby-Smith was born at this site at 12 Aviles Street.

14. St. Francis Barracks
This site is now headquarters for the Florida Military Department. It includes the original coquina walls of the Franciscan monastery and convent that operated here when Maria came to her St. Francis Street home. The British enlarged the structure for military barracks. The St. Francis Street location has been used for military purposes since 1763.

15. St. Francis Street House (Oldest House)
The oldest part of the house at 14 St. Francis Street was built in the early 1700s as a two-room, one-story coquina structure with tabby floors. The second story and fireplace were added after 1775. In 1918 the St. Augustine Historical Society purchased it and today maintains it as an outstanding house museum. The house is listed in the *National Register of Historic Places*.

16. St. George Street House
On the southeast corner of St. George Street and Artillery Lane, this site from *Maria* is today empty again.

17. St. Peter's Church

Mary Evans Fenwick and Joseph Peavett were married in the old Spanish church, now renamed St. Peter's. At present the site, opposite the Convent of the Sisters of St. Joseph on St. George Street, is vacant.

18. Spanish Hospital

A building constructed in 1956 by the State of Florida Restoration Commission to represent the eighteenth-century hospital occupies the site.

19. Tolomato Cemetery

Formerly Spanish Campo Santo Cemetery, this site would be able to tell as many stories as the Castillo if it were to talk. One interesting tale in *Maria* speaks of sentiment and perhaps superstition. Alonso de Cárdenas was an early Spanish governor who was buried in Campo Santo Cemetery. When Spanish families evacuated St. Augustine in 1763, in the face of British occupation, Governor Cardenas' bones were taken from the cemetery to the boat that would carry some of the last Spanish families away.

This burying ground behind Tolomato Chapel near the Treasury Street property of Don Juan McQueen is where McQueen is buried, as recorded in the Parish Register of the St. Augustine Cathedral. Maria and Joseph Peavett, John Edward Tate (Maria's foster son), and Father Miguel O'Reilly (Don Juan McQueen's confidant) are also buried there. Although the cemetery is closed to the public, you can see some markers from the sidewalk. It is located on Cordova Street, next to the Old Drug Store.

20. Ximénez–Fatio House

Located at 20 Aviles Street, the Society of Colonial Dames preserves Louisa Fatio's inn, which was featured in *Margaret's Story*. Tours focus on the way of life when Louisa owned the inn.

The following northeast Florida areas from the *Florida Trilogy* (in alphabetical order) are:

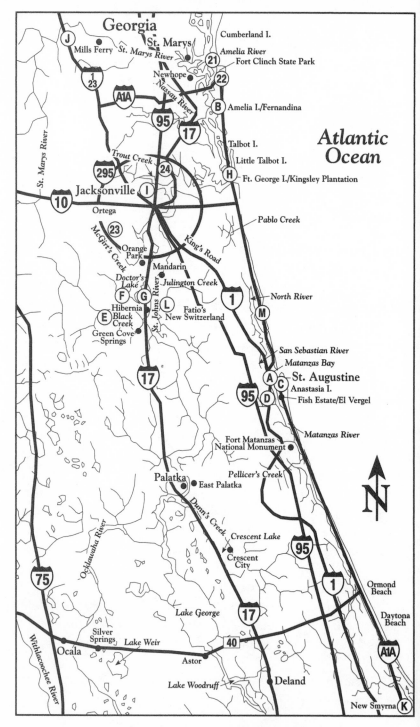

Map 9. Northeast Florida–Points of Interest

B. Amelia Island ❖ Fernandina

Located at the southern tip of the barrier islands, Amelia was named for the unmarried daughter of Spain's King George II. The island was first colonized by Spanish missionaries. Then in 1702 the English burned and destroyed the fort and mission at Amelia Island on their way south from Charles Town. Known as Queen Anne's War, these hostilities did not end until 1713. Don Juan McQueen's property here (granted by Governor White in 1798) is now Fort Clinch State Park, site of the restored Civil War Fort Clinch. In the early 1800s Margaret's family, the Setons, lived in a large square house in Fernandina on Amelia Island.

21. Amelia River

Eight different flags have flown over Amelia Island, emphasizing the vital role of the Amelia River as strategic access to East Florida. Don Juan McQueen especially knew and loved this access to St. Marys and the waterways he traveled to keep alive his ties with family and associates in Georgia. Starting in 1835, a steamboat, used by the Setons, ran the inland waters once a week from Amelia Island as far south as Picolata. Now part of the Intracoastal Waterway, this river separates the northeast Florida mainland from Amelia Island.

22. Bosque Bello Cemetery

Charles Seton died in 1836 and was buried in this cemetery near his large home in Fernandina on Amelia Island. His wife, Matilda Sibbald Seton, lived another twenty years and in 1856 was buried beside her husband. The Setons were the parents of Margaret Seton Fleming.

C. Anastasia (Santa Anastasia) Island ❖ El Vergel Plantation

Modern-day records show Anastasia Island to contain ten thousand acres and to be twelve miles in length along its Atlantic coast south to Matanzas Inlet. At one time, Maria's friend, controversial land speculator Jesse Fish, claimed to be the only owner of Anastasia. El Vergel, his plantation, was famous for its fine orange groves and was noted by François Michaux after his visit there in 1788. The plantation house described in *Maria* no longer exists. Today (Santa) Anastasia Island is connected to St. Augustine by a bridge that crosses the harbor south of Castillo de San Marcos.

D. "Belle Viste" (Bella Vista)

Lieutenant Governor John Moultrie raised indigo, cattle, rice, and vegetables on his large property on the north side of what is today Moultrie Creek, south of St. Augustine.

E. Black Creek

Boundary of Fleming's Island (south of Doctor's Lake), this creek empties into the St. Johns River.

F. Black Point

Location of Mulberry Grove Plantation to the north of Margaret and Lewis Fleming's Hibernia on the St. Johns River.

G. Fleming's Island ❖ St. Margaret's Church, Hibernia

Readers will want especially to see St. Margaret's, Hibernia, the oldest Episcopal Church in Clay County, which figures in *Margaret's Story*. The congregation at Hibernia Landing on Fleming's Island came into being circa 1840. The first recorded Episcopal visit occurred in 1856 when Bishop Alonzo Potter of Pennsylvania visited the Fleming homestead for confirmation and other sacramental rites. The present chapel, an excellent example of carpenter gothic architecture, was begun in 1875 and consecrated in 1894. Margaret Seton Fleming's funeral in April 1878 was the first service held in this church, which is listed in the *National Register of Historic Places*.

This site is all that stands of the great house at Hibernia. Materials from the plantation were used in the construction of nearby private residences.

Those buried in the churchyard are: Margaret and Lewis Fleming; their children Frederic, William, Tissie, Belle, Maggie, and George (marker gone); Lewis's first wife, Augustina Cortez Fleming; and his parents, George and Sophia Fatio Fleming.

H. Fort George Island ❖ Kingsley Plantation (Los Molinos de McQueen)

Located on Fort George Island at the mouth of the St. Johns is Kingsley Plantation Timucuan Ecological and Historic Preserve, one of the few remaining examples of the plantation system of Territorial Florida. It is the site of the oldest plantation house in the state and is now part of the National Park Service. Restoration architect Herschel Shepard discovered in 1988 that the oldest structure on the plantation is the main house rather than a small building to its rear. John (Don Juan) McQueen, who received the island from the King of Spain in 1791, was the owner of that house.

John Houstoun McIntosh purchased it in 1804 and then sold the plantation for $7,000 in 1817 to Zephaniah Kingsley, who managed it until 1840. Although Kingsley advocated lenient treatment of slaves, he believed that slavery was the best method available to ensure the success of agriculture in the South. Remains of twenty-three tabby slave cabins are located approximately one-fifth of a mile from the main house. Originally there were thirty-two of these cabins, sixteen on each side. Located north of the Mayport Ferry on Florida route A1A.

I. Jacksonville (Cowford)

Long ago this area was inhabited by the Timucuan Indians, who lived along its creeks and waterways. Next came the Spanish, led by Ponce De Leon, and then, in 1564, the French, who built Fort Caroline and established the first European colony in America. The Spanish destroyed the French fort and built a flourishing settlement in nearby St. Augustine in 1565, fifty-five years before the *Mayflower* touched the shores of Plymouth. First known as Cowford, Jacksonville was chartered in 1832 and became a center for lumber mills and exporting. With 841 square miles and a growing population, it is the largest city in land area in the United States.

23. Ortega (San Juan de Nepomuceno)

Ortega was the site of Don Juan McQueen's plantation San Juan de Nepomuceno. Today it is a residential area of Jacksonville.

24. Panama Park (Panama Mills)

Margaret Seton Fleming's grandfather owned Panama Mills at this location. Margaret and Lewis Fleming lived there after the Second Seminole War while Lewis managed the sawmills.

J. King's Road

Stretching north to the St. Marys River and south to a little below New Smyrna, the King's Road was a major construction achievement of the British period. The present highway U.S. 1 generally follows its route.

K. New Smyrna

Dr. Andrew Turnbull's colony was in the area of today's city of New Smyrna, some sixty miles south of St. Augustine.

L. New Switzerland Plantation

Francis Phillip Fatio's grant was described in *Maria* as "one gigantic piece of land . . . north and west of the city on the St. Johns." It was ten thousand acres and figured prominently in *Margaret's Story*. Many members of the Fatio family were buried there. No sign remains of the Fatio plantation buildings in what is now the town of Switzerland on State Road 13, a bedroom community for Jacksonville.

M. New Waterford Plantation/North River

In *Maria*, her North River plantation is described as "a thousand acres of good high land, its buildings, dock and adjoining marsh . . .

some twenty miles north of St. Augustine between Guano Creek and the North River. . . ." Just where the house was is not known. Guano Creek and the North River can be seen west of Highway A1A North as you pass through South Ponte Vedra. New Waterford was in this area. The landscape of scrub oak, palmettos, cedars, and magnolias is almost unchanged from Maria's day.

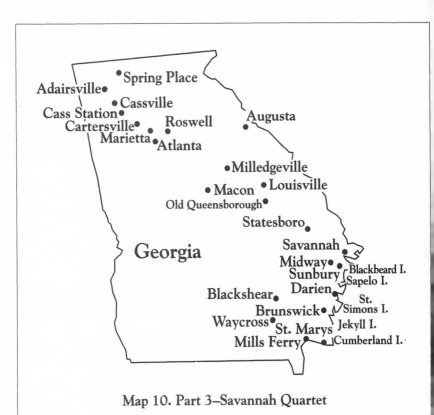

Map 10. Part 3–Savannah Quartet

PART 3

Savannah Quartet

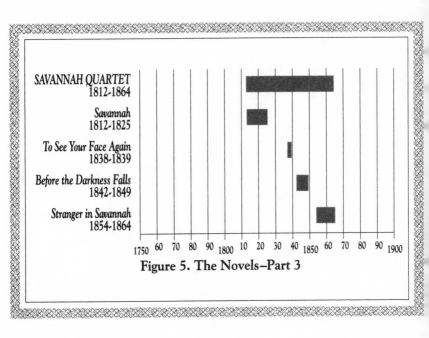

Figure 5. The Novels–Part 3

The Novels

The four novels in the *Savannah Quartet* were published two years apart from 1983 to 1989. Eugenia Price intended to write a trilogy, but because her story line was so strong and she had so many dramatic events to cover (from the War of 1812 to the Civil War), Price gave her readers four books instead of three (the equivalent of nearly four thousand manuscript pages).

Besides the reading enjoyment of an additional novel, other bonuses (among many Price included for her readers in the *Savannah Quartet*) were: two alternating locales—Savannah on the coast and Cassville in the mountains of northwest Georgia; a continuation of the family line that started in *Don Juan McQueen* through McQueen's daughter Eliza; a tie with the world of American politics and the early diplomatic service through W. H. Stiles (the ambitious office-seeking entrepreneur who married Eliza's daughter, Eliza Anne); an intriguing look at the aftermath of the Trail-of-Tears era for north Georgia's Cherokee Indians; and a glimpse into the little-known, long-held relationship between Confederate general Robert E. Lee and the Mackay family of Savannah.

Perhaps the most interesting aspect of the Savannah-based novels is the emergence of a complete family line of major characters who are fictional. In earlier novels the purely fictional characters played minor roles. With the *Savannah Quartet* Price includes enough Browning/Cameron information from her own imagination for a five-generation genealogical flow chart.

At the very onset of *Savannah*, the reader becomes part of the introductions as the fictional Mark Browning meets fact-based Robert Mackay on board Mackay's schooner *Eliza* bound from Philadelphia to Savannah. There is enough time for the reader to get acquainted with each of these men before they reach their destination. Eugenia Price uses this natural kind of introduction to allow her characters to give each other and the reader pertinent family information without disclosing any plot intricacies. As the two men converse, we learn that more than one mystery underlies Mark Browning's background.

Eugenia Price's Browning is a Yale graduate, has just turned twenty, and will inherit the family empire on his next birthday. He is determined to make a new life on his own merit, and for a home he has chosen Savannah because it was his mother's birthplace. He asks Robert Mackay to promise not to tell anyone about Browning World Shipping and the wealth that soon will be his.

The forty-year-old Mackay agrees with one reservation; he has never been able to hide anything from his intuitive wife of twelve years, the former Eliza McQueen, daughter of the late John (Don Juan) McQueen. Although this successful, personable businessman owns a partnership in the Savannah-based mercantile firm of Mein and Mackay, he does not hesitate to tell Browning of his love for his wife and family. The stage is set for an intriguing venture into 1812 Savannah life.

Ever the master storyteller, Eugenia Price chronicles the next fifty-two years through the Browning/Mackay families with perfect ease and balance. In *Savannah* she creates a specter of wealth and commerce without losing touch with the very real forces of good and evil at work in the world that surrounds her characters.

Perhaps the fictional Mark Browning epitomizes Price's creativity as he searches for a sense of belonging. But no more so than the imaginative way she wisely supports Browning's story line with the firmest of foundations—the faith and love of Robert and Eliza Mackay, who so freely and warmly accept him.

Just as the loyal reader has decided that *Savannah* is the very best novel Price has ever produced, the anticipation starts to build. The realization that Eliza McQueen Mackay is the matriarch Price will follow throughout the *Savannah Quartet* comes to the reader even before Robert Mackay's death. After she is widowed, Eliza's strength helps Mark Browning work through his infatuation with her and the emergence of his love for Caroline Cameron. As the plot unfolds, the fictional Camerons of Knightsford Plantation become an extension of Browning's family by blood and by marriage.

According to Price, by the close of *Savannah*, Mark and Caroline's daughter Natalie is a three-year-old "little red-haired vixen." Readers wrote by the hundreds wanting to know what would happen to Natalie. Eugenia Price herself explains in her afterword to the second Savannah novel (*To See Your Face Again*) that "Natalie Browning . . . simply took over this book." Halfway into the writing of *To See Your Face Again*, Price decided to change the trilogy to a quartet. "Natalie's book," the story of her search for the beloved man (Burke Latimer) with whom she survived the sinking of the *Pulaski*, would cover only two years, 1838–39. Additional pages would be needed to carry these families over half a century into the final years of the Civil War. Not only was the length of time a factor but also the geographical distances to be covered.

Burke Latimer, Natalie's fictional love interest, stays true to his own independence and his fascination with America's rugged frontier by moving to the mountainous, former Cherokee Nation territory of northwest Georgia in hopes of establishing himself as a master carpenter and builder. Burke soon befriends an orphaned brother and sister, Ben and Mary (Willow) McDonald, who are half Cherokee and half Scottish.

Through Ben, Mary, Burke, and Natalie, North Georgia would come alive for readers. The fictional characters Eugenia Price created enabled her to tell this part of the South's history; pioneer wilderness cabins could emerge as vividly as the architectural masterpieces of William Jay and Isaiah Davenport in Savannah; and farmhouses, businesses, and churches would be in place to welcome those wealthy, glamorous *real* Savannah families who leave their coastal homes to establish a settlement in north Georgia. The Stiles family—Eliza Mackay's daughter, Eliza Anne, her politician husband W. H. Stiles, and their children—were the first of the Savannahians to move to Cassville in Cass County, building a majestic home they called Etowah Cliffs. The Stileses were followed closely by Eliza Anne's young friend Julia Scarbrough and her husband, Godfrey Barnsley, a wealthy shipping magnate with dreams of building Woodlands, a castle in the mountains.

In the third Savannah novel (*Before the Darkness Falls*), Natalie Browning, like her handsome father, Mark, becomes Price's tie between fact and fiction. Natalie's friendship with the Mackay and Stiles families, her dreamlike marriage to Burke Latimer, her struggle with her brother Jonathan's love for the half-Indian Mary McDonald, and her ongoing resistance to social expectations make Natalie a forceful heroine. This saga of 1840s life in Savannah and Cassville forms a broad and swirling backdrop for Price's tales of antebellum-Georgia life.

Washington politics and western Europe's turmoil during this period become everyday topics as W. H. Stiles wins elections, receives appointments, and temporarily moves his family from Etowah Cliffs to Vienna, Austria, to be near him. This factual aspect gives Eugenia Price additional opportunity to use letters between characters to move the story along.

Stranger in Savannah covers 1854–64 and chronologically parallels *New Moon Rising* (*St. Simons Trilogy*), *Margaret's Story* (*Florida Trilogy*), and the novel now in progress, *Beauty From Ashes* (*Georgia Trilogy*). Consistently and successfully, Eugenia Price shows her writing expertise by describing in fresh, vital ways specific times and events in history from many different locales and perspectives. For example, the War of 1812 is a major event in *Lighthouse, Bright Captivity,* and *Savannah;* and the tragic sinking of the steamship *Pulaski* haunts *To See Your Face Again* and *Where Shadows Go.* With *Stranger in Savannah* the difficult, painful American war between North and South, Union and Confederacy, must be told again in voices of patience, faith, and strength over the emotional waves of anger, confusion, and grief that divided families more harshly than they splintered a nation.

Throughout the Savannah-based novels, Eugenia Price used soundly based research of the period to create the families and their surroundings. Her characters are believable whether they are cultivated Savannahians, upcountry pioneers, or complete "strangers."

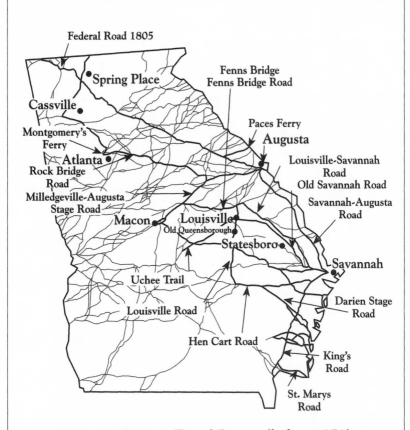

Federal Road 1805

Spring Place

Cassville

Montgomery's
Ferry

Atlanta

Rock Bridge
Road

Milledgeville-Augusta
Stage Road

Macon

Fenns Bridge
Fenns Bridge Road

Paces Ferry

Augusta

Louisville-Savannah
Road
Old Savannah Road

Savannah-Augusta
Road

Louisville
Old Queensborough

Statesboro

Savannah

Uchee Trail

Louisville Road

Darien Stage
Road

Hen Cart Road

King's
Road

St. Marys
Road

Map 11. Georgia Travel Routes (before 1850)
From *Georgia: Early Roads and Trails, circa 1730-1850.*
Georgia Department of Transportation.

CHAPTER 8

People and Places

The *Savannah Quartet* is packed with multiple story lines and subplots. These four Eugenia Price novels cover a period of fifty-two years from 1812 to 1864. The two major family lines are the Mackays, who are based on historical characters, and the Brownings, who are fictitious. The two primary settings are in Georgia—Savannah on the coast, and Cassville in the mountainous northwestern part of the state.

While in Part 1, people and places are grouped by plantations, and Part 2 is organized in the chronological order of the Florida novels, here in the third part, the main characters are presented by family and through the houses of their prominent friends. *Savannah* actually is a continuation of *Don Juan McQueen*, whose main character John (known as Don Juan) McQueen died and was buried in his adopted St. Augustine in 1807. McQueen's family remained in Savannah, giving Eugenia Price an ideal group of "real" people with whom her fictional hero Mark Browning of Philadelphia could become permanently involved.

The McQueen/Mackay Family

Of the five children born to John and Anne Smith McQueen, only the older two, John Jr. (b. 1773) and Eliza Anne (b. 1778), continue into the Savannah-based novels. The McQueen's third child, Alexander, died when he was eight years old (1789); the younger two, William and Sallie, married and had children but do not appear in the *Savannah Quartet*. Almost two years after Don Juan's death in Florida, Anne died in Savannah and was buried there at Colonial Cemetery.

In 1810, the year following his mother's death, John McQueen, Jr., married his cousin and childhood sweetheart, Margaret Cowper, daughter of his mother's older sister Mary Smith (Mrs. Basil) Cowper of Jamaica. Margaret was born in 1777 at the Grange Plantation on the Savannah River. During that time, Anne McQueen and John Jr. lived with the Cowpers while John McQueen, Anne's Patriot husband (later called Don Juan McQueen) was held captive by the British. It was at the Grange that the McQueen's daughter, Eliza, was born in 1778. At the close of the Revolution, Basil Cowper, who had remained loyal to the Crown, removed his family to Jamaica and lost the Grange. Later, when Eliza McQueen Mackay's husband bought the house and surrounding 470 acres as a surprise for his wife (c. 1813), Eliza's birthplace once again belonged to the family. In the *Savannah Quartet*, the Grange is located five miles from Knightsford Plantation, the fictitious ancestral home of the Cameron family.

John and Margaret Cowper McQueen lived at Causton's Bluff Plantation, the fertile land on St. Augustine Creek near Savannah that John had purchased in 1802. During the eight years before his marriage to Margaret Cowper, McQueen experimented with crops at Causton's Bluff. The plantation proved to be profitable even though young John McQueen, who lived until 1822, was not a person who naturally prospered at mercantile or planting ventures. One crop that boosted his success was the ribbon-type sugarcane that McQueen brought from Jamaica. After McQueen's death, Margaret left all her holdings at Causton's Bluff Plantation to their nephew

William Mackay, since the couple had no heirs. Mackay was the son of John McQueen's sister, Eliza, and her husband, Robert Mackay.

Eliza McQueen married Robert Mackay of Savannah at her family's home, the Cottage at Thunderbolt, on January 30, 1800. Mackay's mother was the former Mary Chilcott, daughter of Godfrey Malbone of Newport, Rhode Island. Robert Mackay's father, the senior Robert, moved to Augusta in 1770 and established what was known during the Revolution as McKay's [sic] Trading Post. It was located in a 1750 inn called the White House, which stands today as the oldest house in Augusta at 1822 Broad Street.

Augusta is the Richmond County seat in northeast Georgia on the Savannah River, 110 miles northwest of Savannah. Its origins are with Fort Augusta, which Oglethorpe established in 1735 on the site of a Cherokee Indian trading post. The community incorporated as a town in 1798 and as a city in 1817. During the Civil War, Augusta's factories turned out military supplies for the Confederacy.

Robert Mackay, an only child, was educated in Scotland. Before his marriage to Eliza McQueen in 1800, he had become a partner in a Savannah mercantile firm with Scotsmen Alexander and William Mein. He rose quickly as the firm of Mein and Mackay prospered. Thus the Mackays of Savannah mingled with the business and social elite of that town and prominent political figures and planters along the coast and throughout the young nation.

Eliza Mackay was well respected and much beloved by her husband and family. The Mackay children were: Robert (Robbie), who was born in 1801 and died in 1804; Mary Anne, Margaret, and a second son named Robert, who were not used in the novels; William Mein, Jack, Eliza Anne, and Kate, who in 1812 were ages 8, 7, 4, and 2 respectively; and Sarah (Sallie), who was born in January 1816.

Robert Mackay was a graceful, cheerful, handsome man who loved his Independent Presbyterian Church, his city of Savannah, his country, his work, and most of all his family. Mackay was especially close to Judge T. U. P. Charlton, who was an alderman, lawyer, and judge. Charlton and Mackay were appointed to the

Vigilance Committee for the protection of Savannah (c. 1813). Concerns over the possibility of a British attack had provoked out-breaks of violence, fires, and general uneasiness. Mackay confided business concerns with Charlton and valued his counsel. Mackay was truly a dedicated citizen whose list of friends reads like a Savannahian social register of the day. This family was indeed an excellent choice to welcome Mark Browning into their home. Through Robert and Eliza Mackay, Browning found stability and belonging. Robert Mackay died in 1816, and the stories of the McQueen/Mackay line survived through Eliza, the children, and their friends.

William Mein Mackay married Virginia Sarah Bryan. Her father, Joseph Bryan, served in the U.S. Congress from Georgia. Upon leav-ing political life, Bryan had married Delia Forman of Maryland and they built Nonchalance, a plantation home on Whitmarsh Island at Savannah. Virginia Sarah was born in 1810. Joseph Bryan died in late fall of 1812. William planned to settle at Causton's Bluff Plantation, the home he inherited from uncle John McQueen's widow, Margaret. Tragically, his wife, Virginia, infant son (William), and three-year-old daughter (Delia Bryan) drowned when the *Pulaski* sank in 1838.

The Mackay daughters Kate and Sallie never married and lived with their mother, Eliza, in Savannah. Jack Mackay stayed with the military after attending West Point and was a close friend of Robert E. Lee. Jack died at his mother's home in Savannah in 1848 after a long illness.

In 1832, Eliza Anne Mackay married William Henry (W. H.) Stiles (b. 1809), a son of Joseph Stiles and his first wife, Catherine Clay, daughter of Joseph Clay, of Savannah. Stiles became a student at Yale College but left before graduating. He studied law, was admitted to the bar, and in 1833, when only twenty-four years of age, was made solicitor-general of the eastern district of Georgia. He served in this capacity until 1836. He then returned to his law prac-tice until 1840, when he visited the Cherokee country in north Georgia on a business and pleasure trip. W. H. Stiles was so pleased with the soil and climate of that section that he bought some of the

Eliza Anne Mackay Stiles. This portrait was painted during her husband's term as chargé d'affaires in Vienna in the late 1840s. (Courtesy of the Georgia Historical Society)

newly acquired lands and built a home called Etowah Cliffs on the banks of the Etowah River in Cass (now Bartow) County.

Stiles was elected to the Twenty-eighth Congress by the people of Georgia, serving from 1843 to 1845, and several times he represented his county in the General Assembly of Georgia. From the completion of his congressional term in 1845 until 1849 he was chargé d'affaires of the United States in Austria.

At the onset of the Civil War, Stiles raised a regiment for the Confederacy, known as the Sixtieth Georgia, and served as its colonel. His regiment was attached to Hayes's Brigade, Early's Division, Ewell's Second Corps, Army of Northern Virginia. When his health failed in 1863, he returned to Savannah and died there on December 21, 1864. His wife, Eliza Anne Mackay, survived him by two years, dying at Etowah Cliffs on December 12, 1866. The village of Stilesboro in Bartow County, near where he settled, was named for him.

Their daughter Mary Cowper Stiles was in love with Savannahian Stuart Elliott, whose stepfather was James Stephens Bulloch, grandson of Archibald Bulloch, Revolutionary governor of Georgia. James Stephens Bulloch married Senator Elliott's widow Martha and then moved to Bulloch Hall, their mansion in Roswell. The Bullochs' daughter Mittie, the mother of President Theodore Roosevelt, was Stuart Elliott's stepsister. Stuart died in 1862 and is buried in Roswell in the graveyard of the Presbyterian church. Mary Cowper Stiles had yielded to family pressure and married the wealthy Savannah widower Andrew Low. She died in 1863.

W. H. Stiles's friend Godfrey Barnsley also moved to north Georgia. A native of England, Barnsley came to Savannah when he was eighteen years old and became a vastly successful cotton exporter. He was the first to ship baled cotton from Savannah to England and eventually owned warehouses in Mobile, New Orleans, and Liverpool and his own fleet of ships. He acquired ten thousand acres in Cass (Bartow) County in the 1830s and moved his wife, Julia Scarbrough, and family there.

Established in 1832, Cass County was named for Gen. Lewis Cass, who had strongly favored the removal of the Cherokee Indians from north Georgia. In 1861 the county was renamed Bartow to honor Confederate general Francis S. Bartow of Savannah, who was killed at Manassas Plains on July 21, 1861. An attorney for Godfrey Barnsley, among others, Bartow became an early Savannah military leader, serving in the Oglethorpe Light Infantry. At his death Bartow was a general (CSA) and had joined Generals Robert E. Lee and P. T.

Beauregard in Virginia at Manassas Plains.

Barnsley had extensive plans for his castle and planted a magnificent formal garden of boxwoods, exotic flowering shrubs, and trees, turning the area into an outstanding showplace. Construction of the castle began in 1844, and Barnsley named the estate Woodlands. Priceless artifacts, including imported furnishings, were purchased, many of which never arrived because of the war. Due to many family tragedies and depredations of federal troops, the magnificent castle was never completed. The property, on Barnsley Gardens Road, is now owned by the W. Earl McCleskey family.

Eugenia Price continues to build and intertwine fact and fiction in an inseparable and realistic fashion. At the beginning of *Savannah*, for example, the fictional Mark Browning is a newcomer and accompanies Robert Mackay on a walking tour, discussing the homes, the owners, and the plans for building in Mackay's lovely hometown.

Many of the mansions that survive today were not designed and built until after Mackay's death in 1816. Of the various calamities that befell homes and other buildings in that period, fire was the greatest danger. The devastating fire of 1820, for example, started among a row of wooden houses near Baptist Square on Jefferson, some of which were as old as the city's founding. Quite a few magnificent homes Price incorporated into the *Savannah Quartet* were built after that period.

Isaiah Davenport House

The Isaiah Davenport House (1820–21), facing Columbia Square on the north side of Columbia Ward, is a classic and beautiful example of the historic architecture and plan of Georgian Savannah. Columbia Square and Ward date from 1799, the same year Isaiah Davenport (1784–1827) left Rhode Island and immigrated to Savannah. He married Sara Clark in 1809, and in 1818 he was elected an alderman and began constructing his residence on Columbia Square. Davenport's dignified, well-proportioned, two-story brick house summed up the American Georgian style during the first decades of the nineteenth century.

Richardson-Owens-Thomas House

Between 1816 and 1819, banker and cotton merchant Richard Richardson had this house built for his residence. Richardson's wife, Frances Bolton, was related by marriage to the young architect William Jay (1792–1837), who was a native of Bath, England. Richardson commissioned Jay to design the house even though Jay was twenty-five years old and living in London. William Jay arrived in December 1817 after the house was under construction and stayed several years, designing and building some of the most distinguished structures in town, including the William Scarbrough House, a branch bank of the United States (for Richardson, its president), and a customs house that burned in the fire of 1820.

William Scarbrough House, Savannah. Designed by William Jay, this Savannah landmark figured prominently in Savannah society. Godfrey Barnsley, who built a large estate in northwest Georgia, married the Scarbroughs' daughter, Julia Henrietta. (Photograph © 1987 by David King Gleason)

William Scarbrough House

William Scarbrough was the son of a wealthy planter of the Beaufort District, South Carolina. Educated in Europe, he moved to Savannah about 1798 and soon attained a leading place in the life of the community, becoming one of Savannah's so-called "Merchant Princes" of the era. In May 1819, William and his wife, Julia, made certain the house was virtually completed in time for a visit from President James Monroe on his Southern tour. Scarbrough was a principal backer of the steamship *Savannah*, the first to cross the Atlantic; President Monroe inspected the vessel and attended a reception in Scarbrough's new house.

In January 1820 a great fire destroyed the commercial center of the city, as well as hundreds of valuable houses. But this house and the Davenport, Richardson, and Telfair houses—all new or still being built—survived, perhaps because they were out of the direct path of the fire, rather than because of fireproof construction methods.

Julia Henrietta, the younger daughter of Savannah's prominent Julia and William Scarbrough, married (1828) Englishman Godfrey Barnsley, a wealthy Savannah cotton exporter and owner of ships. After having eight children, Julia Barnsley became ill with tuberculosis and died in 1845. Her husband had hoped the move to north Georgia would be the cure Julia needed, but she never got to see the grand home and gardens Godfrey planned for their estate, Woodlands.

The William Scarbrough House is on the western edge of the historic district in what is now a commercial area. The last great house to occupy that neighborhood, it faces a thoroughfare rather than a square and resembles the newly fashionable Greek Revival style with the flavor of the restrained English Regency neoclassicism that Jay introduced to Savannah.

Alexander Telfair House

The Telfair House by William Jay survives, with some alterations, as the front portion of the Telfair Academy of Arts and

Sciences. In 1875, Mary Telfair, Alexander Telfair's sister and the last member of the Telfair family, bequeathed the home with its art collection, furnishings, and "books, papers, and documents" to the Savannah Historical Society to administer. It was the first house in Savannah to be designated and preserved as a museum. In the 1880s it was remodeled and enlarged to function as an art museum. Dedicated and opened in May 1886, it has continued to serve as the public art museum of the city, the oldest facility of this kind in the Southeast. The octagonal library-receiving room and dining room on the south and the double drawing rooms, or parlors, on the north remained essentially unchanged in form.

Juliette Gordon Low House, Savannah. Home of the Girl Scouts of America. The Gordon family members were friends of Eliza Mackay. (Photograph © 1987 by David King Gleason)

Juliette Gordon Low House

Juliette Gordon Low's birthplace in its first form was completed about 1820 for the jurist James Moore Wayne (1790–1867), at that time mayor of Savannah and later a U.S. Supreme Court justice. Wayne sold it in 1831 to his niece and her husband, William Washington Gordon I (1796–1842), grandparents of Juliette (Daisy) Gordon, who was born here in 1860. The property remained in the Gordon family until 1953, when the Girl Scouts purchased the house to restore as a memorial to the founder of girl scouting and as a center for girl scout activities. The furnishings represent the era of Juliette Gordon's youth in the 1870s and 1880s before she married. The house stands at the corner of Bull Street and Oglethorpe Avenue, facing the historic Independent Presbyterian Church and the landscaped median of the avenue, in Percival Ward, just south of Wright Square.

Andrew Low House

When Juliette Magill Gordon married William Mackay Low in December 1886, Willie Low had inherited this house from his father, Andrew, who built it in 1848–49 for his first wife, Sarah Cecil Hunter Low (d. 1849). Their architect is believed to have been John S. Norris (1804–76) of New York City, who first came to Savannah to supervise construction of the granite U.S. Custom House at Bull and Bay streets.

Andrew Low was one of the most substantial citizens in Savannah and one of the wealthiest men in the British Empire. He remained a British subject with strong ties to England and kept a residence in Liverpool, an important focus of his business. Mary Cowper Stiles Low was Andrew Low's second wife and Willie Low's mother. Mary Cowper was the daughter of Eliza Anne Mackay and W. H. Stiles of Savannah and Cassville. After Mary Cowper Stiles Low died, Andrew Low was alone.

Mary Cowper Stiles. She married older, wealthy Andrew Low, in spite of her lifelong love for Stuart Elliott, in order not to displease her parents. (Courtesy of the Georgia Historical Society)

Andrew Low. Low was said to have been the wealthiest man in Savannah. He remained a British citizen but loved Savannah so much he left instructions to be buried there after his death in England late in the nineteenth century. (Courtesy of the Georgia Historical Society)

Andrew Low died in 1886, bequeathing his fortune and the house to Willie just months before his wedding to Juliette Gordon. Willie died in 1905, leaving Juliette Gordon Low this house where, during a sojourn in Savannah, she founded the Girl Scouts of the U.S.A. on March 12, 1912. Juliette Low died in this house in 1927, and the next year her heirs sold the property to the National Society of Colonial Dames in the State of Georgia as its headquarters and house museum. (The first president of the society was Juliette Gordon Low's mother, Mrs. William Washington Gordon II, and Juliette Low was a charter member.)

Green-Meldrim House

The Green-Meldrim House in Savannah is the most outstanding Gothic Revival house in Georgia and perhaps in the South. Here on Madison Square, in late December 1864, Maj. Gen. William Tecumseh Sherman ended his March to the Sea through Georgia, staying more than a month as the guest of Charles Green, a British subject and partner of Andrew Low. This elaborate house, completed in 1853 according to the design of John S. Norris of New York City and Savannah, cost $93,000 to construct and was possibly the most expensive house built in antebellum Savannah. When completed, it had virtually every amenity, including indoor plumbing. Charles Green died in 1881, and the house passed to his son, Edward. In 1892, Judge Peter Meldrim purchased the property, and it belonged to the Meldrim family until the adjacent St. John's Episcopal Church acquired it for its parish house in 1943. Occupying an entire trust lot extending west to Whitaker Street, the house, its gardens, and trees are an integral part of Madison Square.

The Browning/Cameron Family

The biographical material of Eugenia Price's fictional characters sounds remarkably true. Indeed, they became real in Price's imagination, and to readers they are undistinguishable from her characters who are based on historical people. The fiction line for the *Savannah Quartet* begins with Mark Browning.

When Philadelphia-born Mark Browning was three years old, his mother died and his father's spinster sister Natalie ("Aunt Nassie") took him in to live with her. Mark's father, acting on his severe grief, left Philadelphia the day after his wife's funeral and eventually died at sea. Mark's aunt died a month after his father's death. It was then, in 1812, after he had graduated from Yale, that Browning decided to go to Savannah and make a new life for himself. After all, one of the few things he knew about his beautiful mother, whose portrait he took with him, was that she was from

Portrait of an Unknown Man, *a reproduction of a painting that hangs in Savannah's Davenport House. The painting inspired Price's concept of Mark Browning, the central character of the* Savannah Quartet. *This house was also the model for the home Browning built for his family. Browning serves as a fictional connector for the Stiles-Gordon-Low families of Savannah and North Georgia. (Courtesy of the Davenport House Museum)*

Savannah. Mark lived with the Robert Mackay family, and after opening his successful mercantile office on Commerce Row, he married Caroline Cameron. They and their two children, Natalie and Jonathan, resided in the Browning Mansion on Reynolds Square in Savannah, which was designed by Isaiah Davenport. Mark inherited Browning World Shipping, and when Jonathan joined him as a partner, the Savannah mercantile firm became Browning and Son.

Eugenia Price tells us a bit more information about Mark's parents. Young Melissa Cotting was selling vegetables when she and the handsome Mark Browning, Sr., met in Savannah. They fell in love during his visit to that city. Romantically, she left on a ship with Browning (c. 1787), and they were married when they arrived in Philadelphia. Browning's sister Natalie trained Melissa in social graces and the ways of the wealthy.

Mark Browning, Sr., did not have a good relationship with his own father, but he still inherited the family business, Browning World Shipping. When Melissa died, Browning left Philadelphia. Until his death eighteen years later, he saw his only son, Mark, less than once a year. Browning was drowned off the Bahama Islands during a storm (c. 1810).

Mark Browning's aunt Natalie reared him by herself after his mother's death (c. 1795). He and his parents lived in the Browning mansion on Locust Street in Philadelphia, where Aunt Nassie and Mark Sr. had grown up. Their father had established Browning World Shipping and the Brownings were a socially prominent family. After Melissa's death and the speedy departure of Nassie's brother, the dear woman taught and cared for Mark Jr.

Mark Browning's wife, Caroline Cameron, was an only child and orphaned when her parents died in an epidemic. She lived with her father Jonathan's parents, Jonathan and Ethel Cameron, at Knightsford Plantation on the Savannah River. She married Robert Mackay's friend, Mark Browning on June 1, 1820. The Brownings had two children, Natalie and Jonathan.

Caroline Cameron Browning's beloved grandfather Jonathan Cameron owned the grand Knightsford Plantation. Unfortunately, his wife, Ethel, bitterly loathed and resented this well-respected

Savannah planter. The firm of Mein and Mackay handled the Knightsford factoring business and also acted as go-between for Cameron with his illegitimate son Osmund Kott, who was black-mailing him. Cameron died and was buried at Knightsford in 1818. Ethel died of a stroke around 1825 and also was buried at Knightsford.

Mark and Caroline Browning named their daughter Natalie for Mark's aunt "Nassie" who had reared him in Philadelphia. Young Natalie Browning was on the ship *Pulaski* when the boilers explod-ed. A fictional character in *To See Your Face Again*, she had been with William Mackay's wife and children when they were lost at sea.

Natalie eventually married the young man with whom she was shipwrecked, Burke Latimer, another nonhistorical character from Price's fertile imagination. Her family's good friend William Mackay, attempting to shake his grief over losing his entire family on the *Pulaski*, searched for and found Latimer in Cass County, Georgia. He was living with a young Indian brother and sister who were the orphaned children of Cherokee Indian Green Willow and Scottish Tom McDonald. The children, Mary and her older brother Ben, had been on their own since she was eleven and he was fifteen. They actually lived in a cave less than a mile from New Echota. Mary received less education at the Moravian Mission at Spring Place than her brother but still could read, write, and cipher. She married Jonathan Browning of Savannah, and they were living with his par-ents when their two children were born.

Burke Latimer had been hired by Charles Byrom to construct a store at New Echota. Byrom was realistic about the problems among Cherokee Indian stragglers and settlers as they were forced to remove from their Cherokee Nation capital. Working on the con-struction of Byrom and Kirkham's new general store was Burke Latimer's way to earn enough money for another horse. Then he could easily let Ben and Mary McDonald travel with him. Their cave near New Echota was approximately twenty miles from the growing town of Cassville.

Burke Latimer learned that Fred Bentley was the "brainiest" and "best" lawyer in Cassville. Bentley was a vital contact for procuring important construction jobs, and with the influx of settlers, Latimer wanted to build fine homes for those who could afford them.

The marriage of Natalie Browning and Burke Latimer strengthens the fiction line and broadens the reach of the *Savannah Quartet* into north Georgia. It is ironic that a factual family reference to north Georgia could foreshadow things to come—a day when Savannahians would live on the Cherokees' land.

Indeed—and now returning to Price's historical thread—ten years before his death in 1848, Capt. Jack Mackay, son of Eliza and Robert Mackay, completed his land survey for the federal government at New Echota. He and other officers bivouacked in the comfortable, well-built two-story house that had belonged to Chief Elias Boudinot before the treaty that resulted in the Cherokees' forced removal from Georgia.

Boudinot was the editor of the bilingual national newspaper, *Cherokee Phoenix* (1828–34), published at New Echota. His death in 1839 came as a result of his role in negotiating the 1835 treaty with the United States. He received his early education at the Moravian Mission at Spring Place, New Echota, and was a graduate of Andover Theological Seminary in Connecticut. His wife, Harriet Ruggles Gold Boudinot of Cornwall, Connecticut, died at New Echota and was buried there in the Indian Cemetery.

Eugenia Price's fictional characters demonstrate the realism in her writing. Her "creations," the people from her rich imagination, are based on careful research and study of the era and the location. Jonathan Browning, the son of Caroline and Mark Browning, married Mary (Merry) Willow McDonald. They had two children, a daughter Willow and a son Ben. Jonathan was a partner in the mercantile business with his father when he joined the Chatham Artillery. He was a lieutenant during the Civil War and died in April 1862 from wounds received defending Fort Pulaski against Union bombardment. He was buried in the new part of Laurel Grove Cemetery with other Confederate soldiers.

Willow Browning, the daughter of Mary and Jonathan Browning and grandchild of Caroline and Mark Browning, was born in Savannah (c. 1849). She enjoyed dancing and was well-loved by the Brownings and their friends. Because she did not have strong Indian features, Willow was accepted readily by the social set.

Bending Willow (Ben) Browning was born to Mary and Jonathan Browning in May 1860. He inherited strong Indian features, greatly resembling Mary's Indian brother, Ben. Although Mary was more like her Scottish father (Tom McDonald), the Cherokee blood of her mother (Green Willow) was passed along more noticeably to little Ben.

The fictional thread throughout the *Savannah Quartet* is so well constructed that it blends together with the factual account in a very believable way. Writing about the final days of the Civil War, Eugenia Price makes readers feel as if they themselves are living through the battles. By the close of *Stranger in Savannah*, Price compels both her characters and her readers to push for the war to end. But one dramatic event remains: the last "stranger" must make his way through north Georgia and Atlanta to Savannah.

Atlanta, Georgia's state capital, literally came into existence because of the railroad boom, which was pushed into place during Wilson Lumpkin's term as governor (1831–35). First named Terminus in 1837 as a hub for the state-owned rail lines, then renamed Marthasville in 1843 for Lumpkin's daughter, the town's final designation became Atlanta in 1845. The city was strategic to the Confederacy during the Civil War because of its capacity as a munitions and supply center.

At Camp Rough and Ready, a few miles south of Atlanta near Jonesboro, Union general Schofield successfully isolated Atlanta by cutting rail lines to Macon. Some two months before General Sherman burned Atlanta, he ordered the city evacuated. For those with nowhere to go, transportation was available to the camp at Rough and Ready. General Sherman's Union forces captured Atlanta in September 1864 and burned the city on November 15 of that same year.

In December 1864 Mayor Arnold of Savannah surrendered his city to Sherman's representative, Gen. John Geary, at an appointed place along the Augusta Road. It was along this same route that President Monroe and his party had traveled after his grand visit to

Savannah in 1819. Through Cassville, Marietta, Atlanta, and on to Savannah, there was nothing fictional about those final dramatic scenes in Sherman's March to the Sea.

In the final book in the *Savannah Quartet*, Eugenia Price once again manages to keep her characters attuned to their sense of place and faith and loyalty. Its vivid scenes and portrayals make readers eager to find the factual sites Price used as settings for her fiction just as much as they seek out the places they know to be true.

In Chapter 9 you will read about the Savannah points of interest that appear in Parts 1, 2, and 3. Some of the information on the historic homes is repeated from the People and Places chapters, so readers can use the maps without the frustration of searching back through earlier chapters.

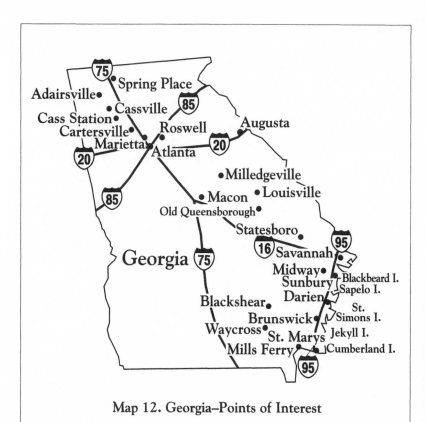

Map 12. Georgia–Points of Interest

CHAPTER 9

Points of Interest

Savannah was originally part of a royal grant made in 1673 by Charles II to the Lords Proprietors of Carolina. In June 1732 King George II transferred the rights to these lands to a group of trustees led by James Edward Oglethorpe. Oglethorpe assembled the original band of settlers who reached the site of Savannah in January 1733.

In the assignment of land to the individual colonists, Oglethorpe granted each freeholder fifty acres of land, but the plan of the inner city of Savannah revolved around its squares, town lots, and wards. Originally the town consisted of four wards, laid out in two rows along the top of Yamacraw Bluff.

To the south of Savannah, Oglethorpe laid out the towns of Darien (New Inverness) and Frederica (on St. Simons Island). Three other coastal Georgia towns—Sunbury, Hardwick, and Brunswick—were laid out by others but with similar plans after Oglethorpe returned to England.

A. Savannah

Savannah is the county seat of Chatham and is the first, the richest, and the busiest seaport in Georgia. Savannah is named for the tidal river on which Oglethorpe founded the original settlement in 1733. By 1851, Oglethorpe's first four squares had grown to twenty-four and the architecture reflected the British heritage that became a tradition. Social, cultural, and business ties with England were strong. Savannah's importance to the cotton and rice planters of the South is evidenced in the Eugenia Price novels. The *Savannah Quartet* reinforces and defines the charm and significance of Oglethorpe's colony-turned city.

1. Battersby–Hartridge House

The Battersby-Hartridge House was built in 1852 for William Battersby, an English citizen and Savannah cotton merchant who was associated with Andrew Low. The designer could have been John S. Norris, a New Yorker who designed the neighboring Andrew Low House. The house faces the Low House front garden and Lafayette Square, and has one of the few surviving original garden plans in Savannah. Battersby and his wife, Sarah Hartridge of Savannah, lived in the house until after the Civil War. Located at 119 E. Charlton Street.

2. Bethesda Orphanage (*See* Map 14)

Charles Wesley and James Edward Oglethorpe were the first to pose the idea of this orphanage. The Rev. George Whitefield raised funds, secured the land, laid the first brick on March 25, 1740, and welcomed 61 children to their new home on November 3, 1740. Bethesda (house of mercy) was built on a grant of five hundred acres Reverend Whitefield obtained in 1739 from the Trustees of the Colony of Georgia. The fictional character Osmund Kott grew up there. The orphanage is off Whitfield Avenue on Ferguson.

3. Chatham Academy

The first public secondary school in the city of Savannah, Chatham Academy was chartered in 1788 and opened in 1813. One of the city's oldest and most prestigious benevolent organizations, the Union Society, was largely responsible for establishing Chatham Academy. The building complex housed the first library, the Union

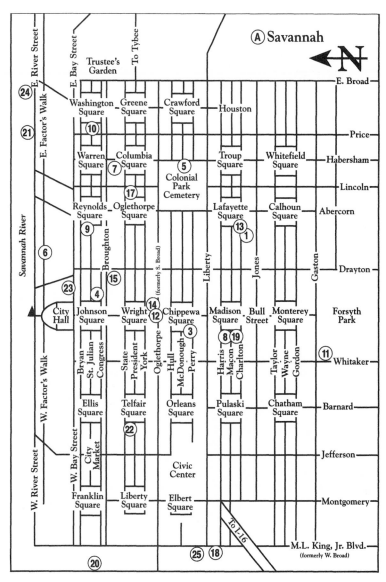

Map 13. Savannah, Georgia—Points of Interest

A. Savannah
1. Battersby-Hartridge House
2. Bethesda Orphanage (see Map 14)
3. Chatham Academy
4. Christ Episcopal Church
5. Colonial Park Cemetery
6. Cotton Exchange ∗ Factors Walk ∗ Commerce Row
7. Davenport House
8. Green-Meldrim House
9. Habersham House ∗ Browning House Site
10. Hampton-Lillibridge House
11. Hodgson Hall ∗ Georgia Historical Society
12. Independent Presbyterian Church
13. Andrew Low House
14. Juliette Gordon Low House
15. Mackay House Site
16. Old Jewish Cemetery (see Map 14)
17. Richardson-Owens-Thomas House
18. Roundhouse Complex Railroad Museum
19. St. Johns Episcopal Church
20. Scarbrough House
21. Ships of the Sea Museum
22. Telfair Academy of Arts
23. Washington Guns
24. Waving Girl
25. Visitor's Center

Society, and the present Board of Education. It is located at Chippewa Square.

4. Christ Episcopal Church

Adrian Boucher was the French designer of the City Exchange (late 1790s) and of the second building to house Christ Church in Savannah. The first church burned and this second attempt was leveled by a hurricane in 1804. Because of his liberal views, Boucher was forced to leave Savannah before ever seeing the church completed. He was known to entertain free blacks in his home and for that he was pressured to move on.

John Wesley's parsonage in Savannah was the original gathering place of Christ Church congregation (1736–37). This most prestigious and influential church on Johnson Square served as the center for the twelve Georgia parishes in colonial days and was designed by James Hamilton Couper of St. Simons Island. The present church was rebuilt after the fire of 1889. In addition to Wesley, this church had as minister George Whitefield, the great evangelist and founder of Bethesda Orphanage in Savannah. Its address is 28 Bull Street.

5. Colonial Park Cemetery

Used as a burial ground from 1750 to 1853. Among the Eugenia Price characters buried here are Anne Smith McQueen; her parents, Mr. and Mrs. John Smith; her son John McQueen (Jr.); Robert and Eliza McQueen Mackay's son John (Jack) Mackay; James Gould's wife, Janie Harris; and other members of the Harris and Bunch families. Located at Oglethorpe and Abercorn streets.

6. Cotton Exchange ❖ Factors Walk ❖ Commerce Row

The price of cotton once was set here for the entire world. Designed by Boston architect William Gibbons Preston, the Old Savannah Cotton Exchange is believed to be one of the few structures in the world erected over an existing public street (1885–87). Factors Walk or Commerce Row was the center of commercial activity when "cotton was king." Ornate iron bridgeways connect offices once used by cotton factors or merchants.

Green-Meldrim House, Savannah. This house served as Sherman's headquarters when the city was surrendered to him in December 1864. (Photograph © 1987 by David King Gleason)

7. Davenport House

Construction on this elegant home in the Federal Style was completed in 1815 by Rhode Island master builder Isaiah Davenport. It is owned by the Historic Savannah Foundation. Hanging in this house is the handsome portrait of an unidentified man Eugenia Price used as her model for fictional character Mark Browning. Located at 324 E. State Street.

8. Green–Meldrim House

This home is used now as the Parish House of St. Johns Episcopal Church. Completed in 1853, it is a marvelous example of Gothic Revival architecture and was the headquarters of Gen. William Tecumseh Sherman during the Civil War. Located at 327 Bull Street.

9. Habersham House ❖ Browning House Site

Built about 1789, the James Habersham, Jr., House (also called the "Pink House") is one of the few buildings that survived the fire of 1796. Its stucco walls surround a handsome Palladian window over the entrance and, on the interior, a beautiful Georgian stairway.

Mark Browning's house was, of course, fictional, but the site Eugenia Price used was across from the Habersham House on Reynolds Square. It is occupied today by the Army Corps of Engineers. Located at the corner of Abercorn and Bryan.

10. Hampton–Lillibridge House

Built in 1797 of clapboards, the Hampton-Lillibridge House has a gambrel roof and a high basement and is a fine example of eighteenth-century architecture. This was the home bought for the Harris and Bunch families in *Lighthouse* and is on St. Julian Street.

11. Hodgson Hall ❖ Georgia Historical Society

Since 1876 this library has been a source for historical research in Savannah. The Georgia Historical Society is one of the oldest historical organizations in the country (1839). Mayor Richard D. Arnold was one of the founders of the Georgia Historical Society. Arnold may be best remembered as the mayor who formally surrendered Savannah to General Sherman in 1864. Located at 501 Whitaker Street.

12. Independent Presbyterian Church

The Independent Presbyterian Church was organized in 1755. The first meeting house stood facing Market Square in Savannah, between what are now St. Julian and Bryan streets, on property granted by King George II. This was the Robert Mackay family church.

Lowell Mason, noted composer of sacred music, was organist of the Independent Presbyterian Church (1820–27) and superintendent of its Sunday school (1815–27). The original church building erected on the present site was designed by John H. Greene of Rhode Island. In 1819 it was dedicated with impressive services that President

Andrew Low House, Savannah. Low, a wealthy Englishman, and his wife were hosts in this house to William Makepeace Thackeray when the Victorian novelist stopped in Savannah on 1853 and 1856 lecture tours. (Photograph © 1987 by David King Gleason)

James Monroe attended. Fire destroyed the church in 1889.

The present church building was completed in 1891. The architect, William G. Preston, followed the general plan of the former structure. It is regarded as a notable example of American church architecture. Located at Bull Street at Oglethorpe Avenue.

13. Andrew Low House

Owned and preserved by Colonial Dames of America, this house was built in 1849. It is furnished in the Late Federal Style. Juliette Gordon Low, who founded the Girl Scouts, came to this home as a bride. Mary Cowper Stiles lived here when she was married to Andrew Low. Located at 329 Abercorn Street.

14. Juliette Gordon Low House

This residence was built between 1819 and 1821. A fine example of Regency architecture, it was designed by the eminent William Jay. The third story and side porch were added later. The house was originally owned by James M. Wayne, one of Georgia's most illustrious public men, until his death in 1867. The Wayne residence was purchased in 1831 by William Washington Gordon (1796-1842), organizer and first president of the Central of Georgia Railroad. Located at 142 Bull Street.

15. Mackay House Site

The Robert Mackay house stood at this site. The original home was torn down and replaced by a business district. Located at 75 E. Broughton Street.

16. Old Jewish Cemetery (*See* Map 14)

The father of Eugenia Price's character Sheftall Sheftall (Cocked Hat Sheftall) was Mordecai Sheftall. This burial ground was established by him on August 2, 1773, from lands granted him in 1762 by King George III as a parcel of land that "shall be, and forever remain, to and for the use and purpose of a Place of Burial for all persons whatever professing the Jewish Religion." The Sheftall plot is approximately one hundred yards from the Georgia Historical Marker. Located at Cohen Street off of West Boundary Street.

17. Richardson–Owens–Thomas House

A magnificent example of the Regency style designed by William Jay, this house was completed in 1819. When Jay came to visit the Robert Boltons in 1818, he was commissioned to design the Richardson home. The Boltons were a prominent family that left Savannah by the close of 1824 because of financial losses. Robert Bolton's wife was the sister of William Jay, and Bolton's sister Frances was married to Richard Richardson. It is furnished and run as a museum by the Telfair Academy. Located at 124 Abercorn Street.

18. Roundhouse Complex Railroad Museum

One of the largest existing pre–Civil War complexes in the

United States. Located at 601 W. Harris Street, one block south of the Visitor's Center.

19. St. Johns Episcopal Church

Built in 1853, this church on Madison Square uses the Green-Meldrim House for its Parish House. Located at Bull and Charlton streets.

20. Scarbrough House

Designed by William Jay, the handsome Scarbrough residence was a center of social life for Savannah. There William Scarbrough and his vibrant wife, Julia Bernard Scarbrough (1786-1851), entertained President James Monroe as a house guest in 1819. Their daughter Julia was married to Godfrey Barnsley. Located at 41 W. Broad Street.

21. Ships of the Sea Museum

One of our nation's finest maritime museums with a superb collection of models, artifacts, books, and ship's chandlery. Enter from 503 E. River Street or 504 E. Bay Street.

22. Telfair Academy of Arts

Designed by William Jay and completed in 1819, this Regency House is both a magnificently furnished house and an art museum with a spectacular collection of American art. The Telfair is the oldest art museum in the south. Located at 121 Barnard Street.

23. Washington Guns

The Washington Guns are aptly named. George Washington sent them as a gift to the City of Savannah shortly after his visit in 1791.

24. Waving Girl

This statue depicts Florence Martus, who waved countless numbers of visitors in and out of the port of Savannah during an almost fifty-year span. The statue is by Felix De Weldon.

25. Visitor's Center

The Savannah Visitor's area houses a helpful welcome center

and the Savannah History Museum. Located at 303 Martin Luther King, Jr., Blvd.

B. Savannah Area

26. Fort Jackson Coastal Heritage Society

Dating from the Revolutionary period, Fort Jackson was an important link in the chain protecting Savannah. The fort was rebuilt in 1842, and today it stands ready for visitors, handsomely restored. Located east of the Historic District on Hwy. 80.

27. Fort McAllister State Historic Park

Situated at Genesis Point, this fort was built in 1861–62 on the south bank of the Great Ogeechee River to protect Savannah. The park is the location of the best preserved earth fortifications of the Confederacy. The fort held strong until December 13, 1864. Located on U.S. 17/GA 25.

28. Fort Pulaski National Monument

Fort Pulaski was begun in 1829 on Cockspur Island (McQueen's Island) to guard the sea approach to Savannah. Maj. Samuel Babcock was the officer to whom Brevet Lieutenant R. E. Lee reported in 1829 for work on developing this federal fort. Not to be missed, this enormous brick structure is meticulously restored and is run as a national monument by the U.S. Park Service. Located on U.S. Hwy. 80 fourteen miles east of Savannah.

29. Laurel Grove Cemetery

Laurel Grove Cemetery was developed due to the overcrowded state of Savannah's old cemetery, now Colonial Park Cemetery on Oglethorpe Avenue (formerly South Broad Street). Laurel Grove was dedicated on November 10, 1852, and is situated on part of the site of Springfield Plantation, which had been under rice cultivation in the early nineteenth century.

Today Laurel Grove has been placed on the National Register of Historic Places for its many splendid examples of Victorian architecture, monuments, sculpture, ironwork, and epitaphs. Many persons

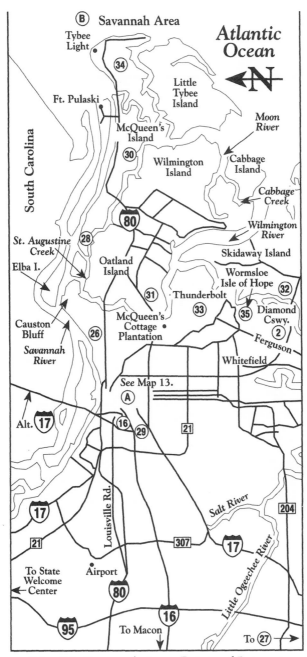

Map 14. Savannah Area–Points of Interest

of national, state, and local importance are buried in Laurel Grove. Interred there are 750 Confederate soldiers, of which 616 are in the Confederate Soldiers' lot. The cemetery also includes a Sailors' Burial area, which was purchased by the Savannah Port Society for the burial of sea captains, officers, and sailors from all over the world who died in Savannah. One notable person buried at Laurel Grove is Juliette Gordon Low, founder of the Girl Scouts of America.

Others interred there from the Price novels are: Eliza McQueen Mackay (lot 486), her son William, and her daughters Kate and Sarah; Andrew and Mary Cowper Stiles Low; Lucinda Sorrel Elliot and her two children; Capt. John Couper Fraser; and W. H. Stiles, whose marker states that his wife Eliza Anne Mackay Stiles is buried at Etowah Cliffs (their home near Cartersville). Located west of West Branch Street on Anderson Street.

30. McQueen's Island (*See* Fort Pulaski)

31. Oatland Island
Once owned by Don Juan McQueen, Oatland Island was used by his family and is located across from Thunderbolt near Fort Jackson, west of Tybee Island.

32. Skidaway Island State Park
This recreational area is on a sea island located six miles southeast of Savannah on Diamond Causeway.

33. Thunderbolt ❖ McQueen's Cottage Plantation Site
John (Don Juan) McQueen's family remained at the Cottage while he lived in Spanish East Florida. Robert and Eliza McQueen Mackay were married at the Cottage on January 30, 1800. Today the area is a shrimping village. It is on the Wilmington River (once Thunderbolt River) along the Intracoastal Waterway off U.S. 80. Take Skidaway Road toward the islands and beaches from Savannah.

34. Tybee Island
The island lies at the mouth of the Savannah River. The lighthouse built in colonial days was the one Don Juan McQueen refer-

enced. That structure's bricks were used in the present lighthouse.

35. Wormsloe State Historic Site

This site is the tabby ruins of the colonial estate established on the Isle of Hope by Noble Jones (1739–45). Jones was one of the first Georgia colonists who came with Oglethorpe. Located at 7601 Skidaway Road 8 miles southeast of Savannah.

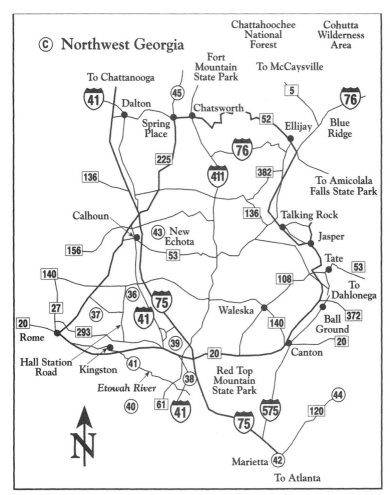

Map 15. Northwest Georgia–Points of Interest

C. Northwest Georgia	38. Cartersville	42. Marietta
36. Adairsville	39. Cass Station * Cassville	43. New Echota Cherokee Capital
37. Barnsley Gardens *	40. Etowah Indian Mounds	44. Roswell
Woodlands	41. Etowah River	45. Spring Place * Chief Vann House

C. Northwest Georgia

36. Adairsville

Just north of this town, Confederate general Joe Johnston established a temporary defensive line and then skirmished with Union general Sherman. The Confederates removed to Cassville five miles south of Adairsville. The federal troops followed and camped along the way at Godfrey Barnsley's plantation. A cavalry skirmish occurred on the grounds of Barnsley's place about two miles outside Adairsville. Located off I-75 at exit 128.

37. Barnsley Gardens ❖ Woodlands

Englishman Godfrey Barnsley established this antebellum estate after he acquired ten thousand acres in Cass County (now Bartow) in the 1830s. He moved his family there from Savannah, hoping the mountain air would cure his wife Julia's tuberculosis. She died in 1845. Barnsley was just completing his Italian-style castle called Woodlands when the Civil War ended his plans. Located off I-75 at Exit 128 at Adairsville. Go west 2.5 miles on Barnsley Gardens Road. Barnsley Gardens is on the left.

38. Cartersville

Originally called Birmingham when it was settled in 1832 by Englishmen, the little hamlet was renamed for Col. Farish Carter at his own suggestion. Carter was jesting, but the name stuck and Cartersville was incorporated in 1850. Only two businesses survived the burning by Union soldiers in 1864. By 1866 rebuilding was evident and the town was incorporated as a city in 1872. Located at I-75 at exit 124.

39. Cass Station ❖ Cassville

The shell of a reconstructed warehouse is a reminder of the once-thriving cotton and sawmill depot at Cass Station and devastation of nearby Cassville in 1864. The railroad did not go through Cassville, as residents believed it would disrupt their lives and those of local college students. Cass Station, just north of Cartersville, was

154

Woodlands/Barnsley Gardens, near Adairsville, Georgia. These gardens were the upland seat of Godfrey Barnsley, the wealthy Englishman whose international business empire was based in Savannah. (Courtesy of Fielding S. Freed)

along the route of the Great Locomotive Chase (1862).

Cassville was laid out in 1833 and was built around the 1837 courthouse square as the prosperous seat of Cass County. Incorporated in 1843, by 1849 Cassville had four hotels, four churches, and numerous businesses. Male and female colleges were incorporated in 1853. But the Civil War brought an end to the booming commerce. Except for a few homes and churches serving as hospitals, Cassville was completely burned in 1864. The county seat was moved to Cartersville, and Cass was unable to regain its prominence or population. Located at I-75 at exit 127.

40. Etowah Indian Mounds

More than four hundred years ago, the mounds were the ceremonial center of an Indian town of several thousand. This state historic site is located off GA 61, 5 miles southwest of Cartersville.

41. Etowah River

The Etowah River rises in Lumpkin County, where it is known as the Hightower. It joins the Oostanaula River ninety-nine miles later to form the Coosa River on its way to the Gulf of Mexico.

42. Marietta

Marietta contains fifty-two sites listed on the *National Register*. A walking/driving tour is available from the Marietta Welcome Center. The Marietta Confederate Cemetery (c. 1863) contains the graves of three thousand men represented by every state in the Confederacy. The Marietta National Cemetery (c. 1866) was used to bury some ten thousand Federal soldiers who fell south of the town of Resaca and the Oostanaula River in the Atlanta campaign. This included Adairsville and Cassville. (Note: *See also* Part 1; *Beauty From Ashes* [forthcoming final book in the *Georgia Trilogy*] follows Anne Couper Fraser as the scene moves to Marietta. Sherman is still in the Atlanta area as that novel closes.)

Just outside Marietta, Big Shanty (Kennesaw after 1870) began in the 1830s as a shanty camp for railroad workers. This town was the location of Camp McDonald, a Confederate training facility established in 1861 by Georgia governor Brown. It would later serve as Sherman's headquarters during operations against Kennesaw Mountain. A strong point on the Western and Atlantic Railroad, the town is best known as the site where the Great Locomotive Chase began in 1862.

43. New Echota Cherokee Capital

The Cherokee national legislature established New Echota as its capital in 1825. This government seat became headquarters for the independent nation that once covered northern Georgia and parts of four southeastern states. Visitors can tour the museum, the reconstructed Supreme Courthouse, the print shop in which the *Cherokee Phoenix* newspaper was printed, Vann's Tavern, and the original home of missionary Samuel A. Worcester.

The cave near New Echota where Ben and Mary Willow McDonald hid (*To See Your Face Again*) was approximately twenty miles from Cassville. Based on factual accounts, this brother and sister were fictionalized by Eugenia Price. New Echota State Historic Site is located on GA 225, just 1 mile east of I-75.

44. Roswell

Roswell King, Sr. (*St. Simons Trilogy* and *Georgia Trilogy*), was the former overseer of the Butler holdings in south Georgia and St. Simons. He and his sons, Roswell Jr. and Barrington, founded Roswell in 1832. Roswell King, Sr., had traveled into north Georgia for the Bank of Darien to monitor their gold-mining interests, and there he bought large tracts of property. He established a village to induce friends from the low country to purchase lots for building summer homes. In time his real estate venture became the town of Roswell.

Of interest to Eugenia Price readers is Bulloch Hall, the antebellum Greek revival house built for Savannahian James Stephens Bulloch in Roswell (c. 1839). Bulloch was one of the earliest investors and a founder of Roswell. His daughter Mittie grew up in this house and was the mother of Theodore Roosevelt. His step-son Stuart Elliott (*Savannah Quartet*) is buried at the graveyard of the

Chief Vann House, Spring Place, Georgia. (Photograph © 1987 by David King Gleason)

Presbyterian Church in Roswell.

45. Spring Place ❖ Chief Vann House

Known as the "Showplace of the Cherokee Nation," the two-story Federal-style brick mansion was built by Chief James Vann in 1804 and features a cantilevered stairway and many fine antiques. Vann improved the education of the Cherokee Nation leaders by inviting Moravian missionaries to teach his people. Vann supported Christianity as a means of progress for the Cherokee. The Chief Vann House State Historic Site is located at the intersection of GA 225 and 52A, 3 miles west of Chatsworth.

From One Reader's Heart

Eugenia Price readers look forward to each new novel for a variety of reasons: the history, romance, suspense, warmth, faith, realism—all of these elements and more greet those of us who venture into the pages of Genie's fiction. No matter our diversity, one thing we all love is a good story.

Then, just as the magic of Genie's storytelling has us captivated, we realize that very soon we will reach the closing words (no matter how slowly we read). At this point our trust in Genie takes over.

So many novelists contrive a happy-ever-after ending or deliberately shock the reader with violence or an unresolved cliff hanger. Not Genie. She knows exactly what her readers want—it is the inside information she gives us in her afterword. At the beginning of this book we looked at the mystique surrounding Genie's loyal following; we touched on her themes of establishing home as a sense of place, enduring faith and loyal relationships as a sense of being. Those characteristics of her novels hold true, but by no means are they (as Paul Harvey would say) "the rest of the story."

Without reservation it is Genie's rest-of-the-story, her after-word, that reestablishes with each novel the bond between her and her readers and makes each story so irresistible. Genie reveals personal details about her own people and places with true honesty and caring. Then she tells us about her research and those who have helped and inspired her along the way. In just a few pages she immerses us in what is fact and what is fiction and how it all came together.

In her nonfiction work *Leave Yourself Alone*, Genie quotes over and over, "What gets our attention gets us." One thing is for sure; in her novels she gets our attention in the afterword and that is exactly what "gets us." So in some way *Eugenia Price's South* is designed to be an expanded version of Genie's afterwords written from this reader's home and heart. This afterword is my "rest of the story."

As a devoted Eugenia Price reader, I have dreamed, for quite a long while, about putting together in one volume those fascinating details surrounding Genie's people and places that are available only to those who own or have convenient access to a vast library and archival collection on the South (or a key to my house). I knew this book would need to reflect personal interviews, local publications, maps, and pertinent information from on-site visits to each of the areas covered in Genie's fiction. After all, Genie has spent more than thirty years writing her novels. Since I have spent a good portion of almost twenty years tracing and retracing her steps, to absorb all I could about her South, it is past time for me to share with fellow readers the results of what, for me, has become a genuine treasure hunt.

Discovering existing evidence of Genie's characters and settings truly enhances her novels. Imagine reading about the Goulds, the Coupers, and the Dodges after you have wandered through the cemetery at Christ Church, Frederica, or viewed the lighthouse from the end of the pier on St. Simons Island. Visualize reliving Genie's stories about the Peavetts, the McQueens, or the Flemings once you have visited Maria's house in St. Augustine, Don Juan's residence on

Fort George Island, or Margaret's tiny chapel near the mighty St. Johns River. Contemplate following Genie's accounts of the Mackays, the Stiles, and the Brownings when you have strolled along Factor's Walk, gazed at the splendor of the mansions on the squares in Savannah, or traveled into the restored capital of the Cherokee Nation at New Echota in north Georgia.

For me, that firsthand experience has been delightful. I also know how it feels to want to see someone or something for myself and, for a variety of reasons, be unable to do so. Therefore *Eugenia Price's South* can serve as travel information for those who are able to make the trip in person, while for others of you, reading this book must become the journey itself.

Although there is no substitute for going back in time with Genie's novels to live out her stories, there *is* an alternative to making a modern-day excursion south. You can read this book and take the "grand tour" with me. My friend Genon Neblett has read each of the Price novels several times; she has located Genie's points of interest with family members and with me on many occasions; and prior to my first visit to Genie's home, she asked me to remember everything so she could feel as though she had made the trip herself. My goal is for each of you to experience Eugenia Price's South through me.

By the time Genon and I planned that first Eugenia Price trip to St. Simons, she and her husband, Ray, had found a wonderful little book about the island entitled *Patriarchal Plantations*, but we didn't know a thing about the author, Bessie Lewis, or the illustrator, Mildred Huie. When we learned that "Miss Bessie" was the organist at the Presbyterian church in Darien, we made certain to stop there first on our way to the island. We called from the church office and excitedly received directions to her house.

Miss Bessie lived several miles outside of Darien at Pine Harbor on land once called Mallow Plantation, property granted by the English Crown to Capt. John McIntosh. In fact, early in the nineteenth century, Reuben King had lived there. (He was the lumber expert James Gould consulted in *Lighthouse* and the brother of

Hampton's overseer, Roswell King, Sr.)

We were anxious to talk with this author about Genie's characters with a specific question in mind about Maj. Pierce Butler of Hampton Plantation. Bessie had written that "in 1771 he married Miss Polly Middleton," daughter of Thomas Middleton of Charleston. In our exuberance over the *St. Simons Trilogy*, we had become more aware of local history. Our mission was to find a possible link between Genie's characters and the mysterious, decaying mansion in Nashville known as the old Middleton/Rutledge house. Some early citizens from South Carolina had built it, but not much more information was available at that time. Miss Bessie told us what she knew and exactly where to look for answers. That project would have to wait until we got home, as we had a more immediate adventure at hand.

"Savannah a Best Seller" was the headline for James Ewing's Book Beat column in the Nashville Banner *(March 12, 1983). Eugenia Price graciously gives a book by local authors a boost while in Nashville autographing her novel* Savannah. *Left to right: Mary Bray Wheeler, Price, and Genon Neblett. (Courtesy of* Nashville Banner; *photograph by staff photographer Don Foster)*

Talkative, brilliant, white-haired Miss Bessie, who decided it had been too long since she had been to St. Simons, put us in touch with her co-author/illustrator friend on the island, Mildred Huie. Before we returned to Tennessee, we had spent an entire day riding in the back seat of Mildred's black Cadillac listening to these two genuine characters describe each and every plantation site on the island. (Bear in mind that this was the same week mentioned in the Preface when we battled gnats to rub tombstones at Christ Church cemetery.)

For some unknown reason Mildred Huie decided to adopt us! The day before we had to leave for home, she smuggled us aboard a senior-citizen tour bus she was guiding to Jekyll and presented us each a tote bag with not-quite-dry paintings of her famous "unendangered species" of island birds and a scene from Genie's novels.

That was just the beginning of years of laughter and fun discovering more and more about the island with each return visit. Some visits brought anxiety—once we went with Mildred to Pine Harbor and discovered that Bessie was desperately ill. Mildred stayed by her side while I courageously drove the "Cadillac" to the island and back.

About a year later, we went with Mildred to a nearby nursing home to see Miss Bessie. We did not know it would be for the last time. On our first visit, Bessie Lewis had given us the only copy she could find of *To Save Their Souls*, the novel about slavery that she had written in the 1930s. Think how proud we were to show her and Mildred, after all this time, a copy of *Chosen Exile*, the book we had written about the Middletons and the Rutledges.

Miss Bessie's house is gone, but you can still see the great oak at Mallow Plantation and read the marker where Capt. William McIntosh is buried. (Follow US 17/GA 25 about 5 miles north of Darien past Eulonia; turn east on a paved road to the bluff at Pine Harbor. The Georgia Historical Marker is a few hundred yards south on an unpaved sandy road.)

Bessie Lewis will be with you as you travel coastal Georgia because this well-loved historian wrote the text for many of the state markers along your way. As for Mildred Huie, look for her island sketches in books and on skirts, umbrellas, murals–everywhere. You can also ask for her at the Left Bank Art Gallery on Frederica Road when you meet her personable daughter, Mildred Wilcox.

Just think, what started as curiosity resulted not only in finding the relationship to the Price characters but also in writing and publishing two biographies. Genie called the first one "a researcher's dream." After reading my early attempts at fictionalizing the Middleton and Rutledge characters, she advised that I stick to nonfiction and asked her history-loving niece Cindy Price to help. Even though we lived in the same city, it was not until then that I met Cindy and her parents, Genie's Nashville-based brother, Joe, and his wife, Millie.

A few years later when Cindy married Mike Birdsong, Genon and I were introduced at the reception as "Aunt Genie's friends." Rather suddenly all other ways to describe us, including our names, faded. Cindy and Mike now live in Kenosha, Wisconsin, with their fine sons, Michael and Joseph. As always, Millie fills her days with creative caring for others and enjoys making any gathering a special occasion. We have shared many good times, but the memory of that moment at the wedding when we left anonymity behind and became honored dignitaries makes me think I should have considered using "by Aunt Genie's friend" on the cover of this book.

Genie's good-natured, down-to-earth brother Joe, who died not long after we met, would have laughed for weeks at such a notion. He adored telling overly enthusiastic Price fans like me that he had *never* read even one of his sister's books. He always made that statement with the kind of mischievous smile brothers and sisters reserve for each other.

I know about that. My modern, fashion-conscious younger sister, Saye Fleming, gets that very same smile when she asks if I remember we are living in the nineties and she doesn't mean 1790 or 1890, or if I have been shopping this "year," or if I would like to tackle something more up-to-date than a spiral notebook and Velvet #2 pencils for my next book. Nothing harsh—just gentle teasing before she shows me the new wardrobe or office equipment or fax machine she pretends she picked up for me at a sale.

Saye, her husband, Grady, and their grown sons, Chip and Matt, are marketing and computer whizzes. A toy for them is a miniature VCR they wear so they can watch movies while they jog. They are all definitely Californians now, but talk of home and Eugenia Price's South keeps us thinking alike.

Through many years of putting together reference books, large and small, I have remembered something Genie said the first time we talked. "Books are not written, they are rewritten," she said, and require discipline and hard work. In addition to those givens, just like a play or any successful production, a finished book represents a great deal more than one person who does the writing. Eugenia Price obviously means what she says. After all, she has twenty million books in print in eighteen languages and always acknowledges her behind-the-scenes crew in each afterword.

Likewise, the final version of *Eugenia Price's South* represents not just my efforts but an incredible amount of work and encouragement from those who helped me. The people mentioned in the Preface and so far in this Afterword have brought me closer to Eugenia Price's South in their individual ways. They are a part of who I am, and for that I am deeply thankful.

A dedicated group of Nashville people stayed with this project throughout and even made me believe they were enjoying the tedious work. Of course I respect their dependability and their accuracy, but the finest gift to me was their unfailing cheerfulness. My heartfelt gratitude goes to Genon Neblett, Linda Wilgosz, Joanne Jaworski, and Charlotte Bell. Charlotte grew up with my children and tries to keep me young; Joanne and I have been working in publishing and on book projects together for years; Linda manages historic and modern commercial properties and also somehow finds herself hostessing my growing family's most important get-togethers; and Genon keeps being my loyal friend and traveling companion no matter how much patience it takes.

These four friends underlined all the people, places, and references from Genie's twelve novels and helped me write, sort, and alphabetize more than five thousand index cards. Genon and Charlotte created specialized lists and proofread for accent marks, cross-references, etc. Linda and Joanne typed computer files from my handwritten manuscript and made changes without complaint.

I will never forget what each one said upon learning I had the opportunity to write a book that meant so much to me. Genon said, "I am so proud of you"; Linda said, "I'll type it"; Joanne said, "Please let me help"; and Charlotte said, "Wow!"

At different stages along the way, family members pitched in. My daughter Marilisa became an expert on *Maria* from the *Florida Trilogy*; my son Jimmy helped make index cards from the 866-page manuscript for *Where Shadows Go*; and my son Shannon asked to work on *Lighthouse* because he still considers the Goulds part of his heritage as he was growing up.

Before I finished writing, our family had more than doubled and my name had changed to GrandMary. The family now includes Marilisa's husband, David Ethridge, and his two daughters, Melissa and Brittany; Shannon's wife, Misty, and her daughter, Britney Leigh-Ann; and Jimmy's fiancé, Rachel Moore; in addition to their extended families and many times that much love. Along with all of these happy adjustments at home, necessary arrangements had to be made with the U.S. Navy for Shannon's leave so he could donate a kidney to Jimmy. My offspring are troopers; despite surgeries, weddings, and new responsibilities, they have focused squarely on priorities. This phase of our lives is already known as simply "the time when Mama was writing the book about Genie."

There are others I wish to thank for their part in this work: for research, field notes, photographs, and permissions—Bob Summer; for map layout and design—Jim Wheeler and Jim Ward; for production of maps and charts—Gary T. Bozeman; and for manuscript evaluation—Nancy Goshorn, Genon Neblett, Millie Price, Annette Tinnin, and Misty Wheeler. Thanks to some who did specific areas of research: on the coastal islands—Joyce Blackburn, Nancy Goshorn, and Eileen Humphlett; on Kingsley Plantation, Fort George Island—Kathy Tilford and Brian Peters with the National Park Service; on Jacksonville—Ben H. Willingham III; on St. Augustine—

Guy Tillis; on Savannah and early Georgia history—J. Clayton Stephens, Jr.; and on north Georgia and Bartow County—Lizette Entwisle, Emily Gilreath, and Shirley Reid.

For continued encouragement and, as Genie would say, "for love's sake," in Tennessee: from Nashville—Barbara Duemler, Ray Neblett, Evelyn O'Lee, Sandra Smithson, Martha Strayhorn, Jean Thompson, Arlene Welding, and Lorraine Whitler; from Clarksville—Faith and Jim Dycus; from Franklin—Gena and Jim Crutchfield, Andy Miller, and Wayne and Jeff Neblett; and from Hendersonville—Annette and Charles Tinnin; in Alabama: from Birmingham—Kelly and Bill Dantzler; and from Gadsden—Florence Daugette and family; in Georgia: from Morrow—Dot and Ed Hickerson; from Union City—Rebie Harper; and from Warner Robins—Mary Lee Wheeler; in Kentucky: from Louisville—Carol Sidebottom; in North Carolina: from Statesville—Betsy and S. L. Collins; and from Washington—Joyce and Tom Dority.

I would like to thank the staff at Longstreet Press who worked together so efficiently toward the completion of *Eugenia Price's South* especially the publisher, Chuck Perry; my editor, Suzanne Comer Bell; and the sales and marketing director, Ruthie Waters.

For an in-depth look at the background of the novels, I would recommend that you read Genie's own stories of research and inspiration in *St. Simons Memoir* (1978), *Diary of a Novel* (1980), and *Inside One Author's Heart* (1992). Not only will you find a record of her journey as a writer, but you will be privy to something deeply personal about the people in her own modern-day world, the ones who appear novel after novel in her afterwords. There is no biographer who could capture in words this author's life and feelings more honestly than Eugenia Price herself.

Genie's closest companions, the ones her perceptive agent Lila Karpf named "Genie's St. Simons Support Group," are Joyce Blackburn, Eileen Humphlett, Nancy Goshorn, and Sarah Bell Edmond. These four live through each and every novel right by Genie's side. I know when the heavy writing schedule keeps Genie, as she puts it, "chairbound," that to receive a greeting card or note or call from either Joyce, Eileen, or Nancy is to hear from Genie as

On the island, Eugenia Price and crew dress in Atlanta Braves' garb to celebrate a winning season. Left to right: Nancy Goshorn, Price, Eileen Humphlett, and Sarah Bell Edmond. (Courtesy of Joyce Blackburn)

well. When Sarah Bell answers the telephone, I know she is in charge of the house and that I have just touched base with the "world of Genie." Sarah Bell's voice exudes warmth and joy; her smile when we met at Eugenia Price Day on St. Simons in 1991 was exactly what I had expected.

Nancy Goshorn has been my steady contact throughout the writing of this book. While Genie was ensconced in the pages and promotion of *Where Shadows Go*, Nance (as Genie calls her) took time from her volumes of research material to arrange a visit for us with Peggy Buchan at Taylor's Fish Camp, managed by Peggy's husband, Danny. With an artist's eye, Peggy pointed out areas of Lawrence and Cannon's Point that I had read about in the *St. Simons* and *Georgia* trilogies but had not seen. As my manuscript pages took shape, Nancy patiently listened to format changes and decisions, stayed in touch with the progress, and encouraged my every step. Her awareness of facts and her sharp memory were welcome additions to this volume. Her friendship is a delight.

Genie refers to Eileen Humphlett as an "overqualified keeper" for her and Joyce. In light of the fact that Eileen is a manager extraordinaire for her own family and for her many and varied civic activities, each time she calls I know she has efficiently "fixed" everything or that something fun is in store, like a celebration or a trip. Eileen, who is gifted with the art of sensible organization, balances all the nitty-gritty for her two authors and makes it look easy.

There is no end to Eileen's thoughtfulness. Of the many ways she has touched my life, one incident that stays with me is when she was the first to call as the 1991 bombing in the Middle East began. Her son Jay was completing pilot school with the Navy in California and missed the "action"; my son Shannon was on the USS *Thomas S. Gates*, the aegis cruiser that was leading the USS *Kennedy* battle group through Desert Storm. Eileen's call was from my own "Island Support Group." It was not the first nor the only time that those dear friends have remembered and encouraged me and my family.

John W. Whitehead said, "Children are the living messages we send to a time we will not see." When all the other sailors from his ship were displaying their ribbons and Desert Storm apparel, Shannon (the same youngster who thought my Mary E. H. Gould tombstone rubbing was from the grave of a family member) was wearing his brand new fuscia tee shirt emblazoned with the cover of *Bright Captivity* and the words *Eugenia Price Day—May 4, 1991*. This is the picture he sent home and of course the one he sent to his special friends on the island.

The Genie/Joyce stories in my family could fill quite a different kind of book, but I must tell you that Shannon helped me see the impact these two have made on our lives. I was called to his school one day when he was in the third grade. The librarian (an ardent Price reader) had requested a conference because Shannon had interrupted story time with what she considered a deliberate fabrication. His lively account of a Saturday morning phone call from "Eugenia Price" that came during his television cartoons seemed obviously untrue to her. It took some fast talking to assure her, the teacher, and the principal that Shannon was not having a problem with reality.

Eugenia Price and Joyce Blackburn, St. Simons Island. (Courtesy of Merriam A. Bass)

Things settled down a bit until a group of parents with Shannon's Little League baseball team overheard his rendition of an Atlanta Braves' baseball game shared inning by inning over the telephone with "Joyce Blackburn." It seemed the coach's wife loved

Joyce's *Suki* books and biographies and just couldn't believe Shannon really knew her. At the next game he put an end to the woman's disbelief with his autographed copy of Joyce's *James Edward Oglethorpe*. That was not long after I had driven him to the interstate at seven o'clock one morning so he could see Joyce before she headed home from Nashville.

Like Genie, Joyce has a special place in our hearts. She cheers me with a delightful brand of humor all her own and is my mentor as a biographer and historian. Her writing challenges me to be a responsive, whole person, particularly her expressive work, *A Book of Praises* (1980).

As you read this afterword you should know that I keep everything. Those who care about me never call me a "pack rat"; in kindness they refer to me as the "archivist." Therefore I have held onto each communication from my cherished St. Simons friends. In the Bible I have used since childhood, I keep a well-worn postcard Joyce sent to me not long after her mother's death. The print on the front is Claude Monet's peaceful *Apple Trees in Bloom*; on the back (knowing I was struggling with a loss she understood) Joyce shared with me two notes her mother had sent her at just such a time in her life: "Christians are like tea; their real strength is not drawn out until they get in hot water." And "Don't be afraid. Just stand where you are and watch and you will see the wonderful way the Lord will rescue you today" (Ex. 14:13). Each time I read Audry Blackburn's notes to her daughter who sent them to me, I realize that not only is Joyce her mother's living message to me and to others in her life, but Joyce's books, like Genie's, are the communication links from their characters to us and to generations beyond this time.

I have dedicated this book to my parents, Frances and O. J. Bray. Because of them I had a love for Genie's people and places long before I read the novels. In the early forties they bought a Reconstruction-era, two-story farmhouse on Campbellton Road in southwest Atlanta. Adjacent to our property was the marker pointing out the Confederate defensive line crossed by Sherman's armies en route to Jonesboro at the end of the Atlanta campaign. That twelve-acre farm was our family home until my second year in college. It was there on walks up the sloping hillside that overlooked the house and down through the towering pines to the spring that I would imagine the activity that fertile land must have seen. In no way did I limit my daydreaming to General Sherman; I loved to think about Indians and pioneer settlers and anyone who might have lived there before us.

I asked my parents endless questions and as a result learned a different area of southern history from each of them. From my father I learned to love quiet and privacy and to respect in particular Indian lore and nature; my mother emphasized political and social skills, devoting endless hours to community service.

He was chief flight dispatcher for the busy Atlanta airport and, as my mother liked to say, raised enough vegetables to feed the Third Army at nearby Fort McPherson. She organized, to name a few, a church, a woman's club, a speaker's club, a YWCA camp for the underprivileged, and the Atlanta Children's Civic Theater.

Two very different people with some amazing things in common—they each collected books and antiques, were staunch Presbyterians for generations back, and were licensed commercial pilots in their teens. (My aviation-pioneering parents seemed almost embarrassed that I was nearly twenty before I decided to try driving an automobile.)

So what does this have to do with *Eugenia Price's South*? Early memories of my late father include north Georgia excursions to the Indian mounds at Cartersville or the area around New Echota and Chief Vann's abandoned house at Spring Place. That was before there were any signs of restoration projects and any talk about the importance of preserving the Cherokee Nation's capital.

As a child I heard my mother's stories of how she flew millionaire R. J. Reynolds back and forth from Winston Salem, North Carolina, to his retreat on Sapelo Island when she was only seventeen. Her sister and brother remember rounding up friends with automobiles so their headlights could mark the runway for her night landings. Mother, always fascinated by Georgia's coastal islands, passed her interest along to me. A massive stroke in 1977 took away her ability to speak, but her eyes shine with delight when I tell her about Eugenia Price's South. It is no wonder, then, that for me Genie's novels speak of home—whether it be the mountains, the coast, or Sherman's armies on the march through the front yard of my youth.

At this writing, I am surrounded by manuscript pages and stacks of research material; Genie's volumes of fiction and nonfiction are before me, tangible reminders of places I enjoy seeing and people, past and present, whom I treasure because of her. This afterword is called "from one reader's heart" not only so I may share my personal journey into Genie's south, but so you will know that, in a collective sense, you and I are one.

Genie consistently expresses gratitude to us, her loyal readers, at the close of each afterword. So let us together, as this book ends, respond to her by saying: "Genie, because of all you give to us and because of the bond we share, it is our turn to thank you from deep within our hearts."

APPENDIX

Cast of Characters

Abbreviations

St. Simons Trilogy
  Lighthouse [LH]
  New Moon Rising [NM]
  The Beloved Invader [BI]
Georgia Trilogy
  Bright Captivity [BC]
  Where Shadows Go [WS]
  Beauty From Ashes (forthcoming) [BF]

Florida Trilogy
  Maria [MA]
  Don Juan McQueen [DJ]
  Margaret's Story [MS]
Savannah Quartet
  Savannah [SA]
  To See Your Face Again [TS]
  Before the Darkness Falls [BD]
  Stranger in Savannah [SS]

The appendix contains a comprehensive alphabetized listing of characters from the Eugenia Price novels. The list is organized by trilogy or quartet (Parts 1, 2, and 3 of this book). Each individual novel is designated by an abbreviation symbol in brackets. A character may have several abbreviations after his or her name, which means simply that the character appears in more than one novel.

Fictional characters are noted with an asterisk. Although they are based on fact, Eugenia Price gave them fictional names. The best examples are the slaves and minor characters who were found in the research as anonymous references. Where only a first or last name was available, descriptive information is provided in parentheses.

For those who already have read the novels, this appendix will refresh your memory at a glance as to the characters covered in any one set of the books. For those who are unfamiliar with the scope of the Price novels, this section will prove a handy reference tool. The sheer volume of characters and references highlights the depth of Eugenia Price's writing. Because of the many printings (both hardcover and paperback), the page numbers vary and were not used.

Part 1 St. Simons Trilogy [LH, NM, BI]
Georgia Trilogy [BC, WS]

Abbott, Agnes Dunn [NM]
Abbott, George [LH, NM, BC, WS]
Abbott, Mary Wright [LH, NM, BC, WS]
Abbott, Richard [NM]
Abraham (Gould slave; "Old Lamp Black") [LH]
Abraham (Butler slave; carpenter) [BC]
Adam (Gould slave; Black Banks butler) [NM]
Adams, John Quincy [WS]
Armstrong, Ann [BC]
Armstrong, Dr. [BI]
Armstrong family [LH, BI, BC]

Banks, Captain [LH]
Barry, Capt. John [LH]
Bartow, Isabella (Belle) Couper [NM, BC, WS]
Bartow, Rev. Theodore B. [NM, WS]
* Bass, Emma and P. D. [BI]
Beauvoir, Mme. [NM]
Beck, Mr. [LH, BC]
Beckwith, Right Rev. J. W. [BI]
Berkeley, Francis Henry Fitzhardinge [WS]
Bessie (Abbott slave; Orange Grove) [NM]
Best, Rev. Dr. William [LH]
Betty (Old Betty; Page slave; Retreat) [BC]
* Big Boy (Couper Ebo slave; later Fraser's groom and fisherman at Lawrence) [BC, WS]
* Bob (servant at Glove Inn; Dumfries, Scotland) [BC]
* Bob (William Fraser's driver; Darien)

[WS]
* Bob (Young Bob; John Fraser's slave at Lawrence) [WS]
Bowers, Mr. [WS]
Boyd, William [LH]
* Bozey (Gould slave; lighthouse helper) [LH]
Bram (Butler slave; Hampton Plantation driver; son of Minda) [WS]
Broadfoot, Mr. [LH]
Brown, Gov. Joseph Emerson [NM]
Brown, Rev. [BI]
Browne, William [BC, WS]
* Browning, Caroline Cameron [WS]
* Browning, Mark [BC, WS]
Buchanan, James [NM]
* Budge, Capt. and Mrs. James [LH]
Buffton, Mr. [LH, NM]
Bul-ali (Bu Allah; Ben-Ali; Spalding Muslim slave at Sapelo) [BC]
Bunch, Elizabeth Harris [LH]
Bunch, Capt. Samuel [LH]
Burr, Aaron [LH]
Burroughs, Mr. [LH]
* Burt (Gould slave; New St. Clair) [NM]
Burton, Braxton [WS]
Butler, Frances Anne (Fanny) Kemble [NM, BC, WS]
Butler, John (John Mease) [WS]
Butler, Maj. Pierce [LH, BC, WS]
Butler, Pierce (Pierce Butler Mease, called Butler Mease) [NM, WS]
Butler, Sarah [WS]
Butler family [WS]

* Ca (Gould slave; daughter of Maum Larney and Papa John [LH, NM, BI]

Campbell, Jessie Caroline Gould [NM, BI]

Cantwell, Helen Gould [NM, BI]

Carlos, Don [LH]

Cater, Benjamin (Ben) Franklin [LH, NM]

Cater family [BI, BC, WS]

Channing, Rev. William Ellery [WS]

Chapman, John [BI]

Clay, Henry [NM, WS]

Clow, Mr. and Mrs. [LH]

Cochrane, Vice Admiral [BC]

Cockburn, Rear Adm. Sir George [LH, BC]

Comochichi (James Gould's Creek Indian guide, worker, and friend) [LH]

Comochichi's squaw [LH]

Couper, Alexander Wylly [WS]

Couper, Caroline Wylly [BC, WS]

Couper, James Hamilton [LH, NM, BC, WS]

Couper, John, Jr. [LH]

Couper, John (Jock) [LH, NM, BI, BC, WS]

Couper, Rebecca Maxwell (Becca) [LH, BI, BC, WS]

Couper, William Audley [BC, WS]

Couper family [BI]

* Crawford, Bubba [BC]

Crosby, Simon [LH]

Crumit, Major [WS]

Cuffy (Couper blacksmith; Cannon's Point) [LH, BC]

Cuffy (John Fraser's driver; Lawrence; son of Muslim Tom) [WS]

* Davidson, Michael [LH]

Davis, John "Toto" [NM]

Day, Jeremiah [NM]

Demere, Joseph [LH, NM]

Demere, Lewis [WS]

Demere, Paul [WS]

Demere, Raymond [LH, BC]

Demere family [LH, NM, WS]

Demorest, Madame [BI]

Dennet, Jacob [LH]

Diana (Butler slave) [WS]

Dick, (Bunch slave; bought by James Gould) [LH]

Dick, (Old Dick; Couper slave) [LH]

Dodge, Anna Deborah Gould [NM, BI]

Dodge, Anson Greene Phelps, Sr. [BI]

Dodge, Anson Greene Phelps, Jr. [BI]

Dodge, Anson Greene Phelps III [BI]

Dodge, Arthur Murray [BI]

Dodge, Cornelia M. [BI]

Dodge, Ellen Ada Phelps Dodge [BI]

Dodge, Josie [BI]

Dodge, Melissa [BI]

Dodge, Norman [BI]

Dodge, Rebecca Grew [BI]

Dodge, Rev. Stuart [BI]

Dodge, Theodore [BI]

Dodge, William E. [BI]

Donne, John [NM]

Drayson, Mrs. [LH]

Drysdale, Alex [NM]

Drysdale, Mrs. [NM]

duBignon, Col. Henry [NM, BC, WS]

* Dundle, Widder [NM]

Dunn, James [NM]

Dunn, Capt. Robert [NM]

* Dusty (Couper slave; Cannon's Point; groom) [WS]

Eagen, A. M. [NM]

* Eddie (Couper slave; oarsman) [LH]

Elizafield [NM]

Ella (Hamilton Plantation slave; "main woman") [WS]

Ellesmere, Lady [WS]

Emma, (Aunt Emma; Couper slave) [BC]

* Enoch (stevedore; worked with Horace Bunch Gould in Savannah) [NM]

Evans, Anna [NM]

Evans, Elizabeth [NM]

* Eve (personal maid to Anne Couper Fraser; originally belonged to John Couper of Cannon's Point; daughter of Fanny [slave] and Roswell King, Sr.; married to Ebo June) [BC, WS]

Fanny (Bunch slave bought by James Gould) [LH]

* Fanny (Couper slave; daughter of Granny Sofy; mother of Eve) [BC]

Flora (Butler slave) [BC]

Floyd, Brig. Gen. John B. [BC]

Floyd family [BC]

Frank (slave described as a coachman and hostler at Savannah auction) [LH]

Fraser, Anne Couper [BC, WS]

Fraser, Clarence Brailsford [WS]

Fraser, Frances Anne (Fanny) [WS]

Fraser, Frances Anne Wylly [BC, WS]

Fraser, James [BC, WS]

Fraser, James William [WS]

Fraser, John [LH, NM, BC, WS]

Fraser, John Couper [WS]

Fraser, Margaret Thompson [BC, WS]
Fraser, Menzies [WS]
Fraser, Rebecca (Pete) [WS]
Fraser, Selina Tunno [WS]
Fraser, Simon the Younger [BC]
Fraser, Dr. William [BC, WS]
* Freddie (Willy Maxwell's house servant) [BC]
Frewin, Capt. James [NM, WS]
Frewin, Sarah Dorothy Hay [NM, WS]
Fuller, Warren [BI]

Gallatin, Hon. Albert [LH]
* Ganshorn, Captain [WS]
Gaylord, Mary Gould [LH]
* George (Lawrence slave) [WS]
Gould, Alice [NM]
Gould, Deborah Abbott [NM]
Gould, Horace [LH, BC]
Gould, Horace Abbott [NM, BI]
Gould, Horace Bunch [LH, NM, BI, WS]
Gould, Capt. James [LH]
Gould, James [LH, NM, BC, WS]
Gould, James III (Jim) [LH, NM, BC, WS]
Gould, James IV (Jamie) [NM]
Gould, James Dunn (Jimmie) [NM, BI]
Gould, Jane (Janie) Harris [LH, NM, BC, WS]
* Gould, Jessie Davidson [LH]
Gould, Kate [LH]
Gould, Mary E. H. [LH, NM, BI, BC, WS]
Gould, Mary W. (Maimie) Green [BI]
Gould, Sister Mary Joseph [NM, BI]
Gould, William [LH]
Gowen, Ann (Annie) Abbott [NM, WS]
Gowen, James [WS]
* Grace (Stevens servant; Frederica) [NM]
Graham, John [LH]
Grant, Hugh Fraser [NM]
Grant, Joseph [LH]
Grant, Dr. Robert [LH, NM, WS]
Grant, Ulysses S. [NM, BI]
* Green, Proctor (worked for Rev. Anson Dodge) [BI]
Greene, Gen. Nathanael [LH, BC]
Griffith, Lt. James [BC]
Grimke, Mr. [NM]
Guy (Couper slave; Cannon's Point) [BC]

Habersham, John [LH]
Habersham, Joseph, Jr. [SA, BC, WS]
Hall, Basil [BC]
Hamilton, Agnes [WS]

Hamilton, James [LH, BI, BC, WS]
Hamilton, Janet Wilson [WS]
Harriet (Butler slave; wife of Ned) [WS]
Harris, Caroline [LH, NM]
Harris, Charles [LH]
Harris, Mayor Charles [LH]
Harris, John Hartley [LH]
Harris, John Mackay [LH]
Harris, Kitty McIntosh [LH]
Harris, Mary [LH]
Harris, Stephen [LH]
Haynes, Lemuel [LH, WS]
Haynie (childhood nurse for Anna Matilda Page King; Retreat) [BC, WS]
Hayworth, Dr. [BI]
Hazzard, Sarah Stewart Richardson [WS]
Hazzard, Dr. Thomas Fuller [NM, WS]
Hazzard, Col. William Wigg (Whig) [NM, BI, WS]
Hetta (King slave; Retreat; mother of Neptune) [NM]
* Higgins, Katy (Kate; Fraser nanny in London) [BC, WS]
Hillary, Christopher [LH]
Holland, Lucy [LH]
Holland, Capt. Park [LH]
Hone, Philip [WS]
* Hop (lumberjack; worked at Mills Ferry; brother to Jake) [LH]
Howard, Rev. Charles [LH]
Howard, Thomas [LH]
* Howsam family [LH]
Humphreys, Joshua [LH]
* Hunter, Dr. [LH]

Jack (Butler Island slave; personal escort for Fanny Kemble Butler) [WS]
* Jackson, Sibby (House maid for Rev. Anson Dodge) [BI]
* Jake (lumberjack at Mills Ferry; brother to Hop) [LH]
Jasper (Gould slave; New St. Clair) [NM]
* Jasper (deaf wagon driver for Dr. Troup of Darien) [WS]
Jefferson, Thomas [BC, WS]
Jenkins, Mr. [NM]
Jimmy (Butler slave; Hampton; bricklayer) [BC]
Joan (Page slave; Retreat; cook) [BC]
* Joe (Gould slave; New St. Clair) [NM]
* John (Papa John; Gould slave; New St. Clair head driver; grew indigo;

Greene [BC]
Miller, Phineas [BC]
Mina (King slave; Retreat; Adam's love) [NM]
* Mina (Couper slave; Cannon's Point; trained as a cook by Sans Foix; given to Anne Couper Fraser) [WS]
Minda (Butler slave; Hampton; mother of Bram) [WS]
Minerva (Page slave; Retreat) [BC]
Minis, Dinah [BC]
Minis, Henrietta [BC]
Minis, Isaac [BC]
Minis, Sarah [BC]
Morgan, John T. [LH]
Motte, Reverend [WS]
* Myrtle (Shaw slave; Dungeness, Cumberland Island) [BC]

* Nancy (Gould slave; New St. Clair; daughter of Ca) [NM, BI]
Ned (Butler engineer at rice mill; Butler Island; married to Harriet) [WS]
* Nell (William Fraser family nurse; Darien) [WS]
Neptune (King slave; Retreat; son of Hetta) [NM]
Newell, Capt. Thomas [BC]
Nightingale, Louisa [WS]
Nightingale, Phineas Miller [WS]
Nightingale, Mrs. Phineas Miller [WS]
Nightingale family [LH, BC, WS]
Noble, Rev. and Mrs. Seth [LH]
Norton, Birdsey [BC]

Oden, Thomas [WS]
Oglethorpe, Gen. James [LH, NM, BI, BC, WS]
Olmstead family [NM]

Page, Hannah Timmons [WS]
Page, Maj. William [LH, BC, WS]
Patterson (John Couper's overseer; Cannon's Point) [BC]
* Peddler Sam [LH]
Perry, Elizabeth (Lizzie) Fraser Gould [NM, BI]
* Peter (Fraser slave; Lawrence) [WS]
Phebe (Old Phebe; Shaw slave; Dungeness, Cumberland Island) [BC]
Phillips, Reverend [BI]
Pinckney, Gen. Thomas [BC]
Polly (Page/King slave; Retreat) [BC]
Pool, Capt. Charles [NM]

Postell, Clifford [BI]
Postell, Mackbeth (St. Mack) [BI]
Postell family [BI]

Quesada, Gov. Juan Nepomuceno de [LH]

Ramsey, Captain [BC]
* Rena (Aunt Rena; Proctor Green's aunt) [BI]
Rhina/Rhyna (Maum Rhina/Rhyna; Granny woman; Couper slave; Cannon's Point) [LH, NM, BC, WS]
Richardson, Jane Gould [LH, NM]
Richardson, Orville [NM]
Robert (King slave; Retreat) [NM]
* Robert (Butler slave; Hampton) [BC, WS]
* Rollie (Fraser slave; Lawrence) [WS]
Rose, Deacon [LH]
Rutty (Page/King slave; Retreat) [BC, WS]

Sallie (Shaw slave; Dungeness, Cumberland Island) [BC]
Sally (King slave; Retreat; Lady's daughter) [WS]
Sally (Aunt Sally; Couper slave; Cannon's Point) [BC]
Sam (Page slave; Retreat) [BC]
* Samantha (Annie Fraser's best friend in London) [WS]
Sancho (Butler slave; Hampton; brick layer) [BC]
* Sandy (Couper slave; Cannon's Point) [LH]
Sans Foix (Couper free person of color; Cannon's Point; chef) [LH, BC, WS]
Scott, Charles [BC]
Scott, Charlotte [BC, WS]
Scott, Sophia [BC]
Scott, Sir Walter [BC, WS]
Seagrove, James [LH]
Semmes, Col. Paul [NM]
Shaw, Louisa Catherine Greene [BC, WS]
Shaw family [LH]
Shays, Capt. Daniel [LH]
* Shedd, Widow [NM]
Sherman, Gen. William Tecumseh [NM, BI]
Siddons, Sarah [BC, WS]
* Sims, Captain (Cap'n) [BI]
Sinclair, Archibald [LH]
Smart (King slave; Retreat) [WS]

Smart brothers [LH]
Smith, Eliza [LH]
Smith, Maj. G. T. [NM, BI]
Smith, Jonathan [LH]
* Sofy (Couper slave; Cannon's Point;
      Eve's grandmother) [BC, WS]
Spalding, James [LH, WS]
Spalding, Sarah Leake [BC]
Spalding, Thomas [BC, WS]
Steiner, John [NM]
Steuart, Angela (Angé) La Coste Gould
      [NM, BI]
Stevens, Capt. Charles [NM]
Stevens, George [BI]
Stevens, John [BI]
Stevens, Rossie [BI]
Stevens, Sarah Dorothy Hay [NM]
Stevens family [BI]
* Stiles, Nancy [LH]
* Stiles, Timothy [LH]

* Tab (Gould slave; New St. Clair) [NM]
* Tapo (Gould slave; New St. Clair) [LH]
Taylor, Archibald [BI]
Taylor, Belle [BI]
* Taylor, Doc [LH]
Taylor, Douglas [BI]
Taylor, Reginald [BI]
Taylor, Will [BI]
Taylor family [BI]
* Thatcher, Harriett [NM]
* Thatcher, Linda [NM]
* Tiber (Fraser slave; Lawrence) [WS]
* Tom (Bunch slave; bought by James
      Gould) [LH]
Tom (Muslim Tom; Couper slave;
      Cannon's Point; oarsman) [LH, BC,
      WS]
Toombs, Sen. Robert [NM]
Treat, Maj. Robert [LH]
Treat family [LH]
Troup, Dr. James McGillivray [NM,
      WS]
Trowbridge, John [LH]
Trowbridge, Rachel Gould [LH]
* Tuesday (Gould slave; New St. Clair;
      daughter of Matty) [NM]
Tunno, Dr. [BC, WS]
Turner, Joseph [LH]
Twining, Nathaniel [WS]

Van Buren, Martin [WS]
Vernon, Tom [LH]

Wardrobe, Lieutenant Colonel [BI]
* Webber, Sam [LH]

Webster, Andrew [LH]
Webster family [LH]
Wesley, Charles [BI, BC]
Wesley, John [BI, BC]
Williams, Lt. Col. Richard [BC]
Winn, Rev. D. Watson [BI]
Wright, Mrs. [BI]
Wright, Maj. Samuel [LH]
Wylly, Capt. Alexander [LH, NM, BC,
      WS]
Wylly, Alexander William [NM, BI, BC,
      WS]
Wylly, Anne Frances [BC, WS]
Wylly, Heriot [NM, BC, WS]
Wylly, John Armstrong [NM, BC, WS]
Wylly, Margaret Armstrong [LH, NM,
      BC, WS]
Wylly, Margaret Matilda [NM, BC, WS]
Wylly family [LH, NM, BI, BC, WS]
Wythe, George [WS]

Part 2   Florida Trilogy [MA, DJ, MS]

Adams, Samuel [MA]
Ainslie, Juan [MA]
Amherst, Gen. Jeffrey [MA]
Anderson, Maj. Robert [MS]
Anderson, Sarah [MS]
Arbuthnot family [MA]
Atkinson, Capt. Andrew [DJ]

Beaumarchais, Pierre [MA]
Beauregard, Brig. Gen. Pierre [MS]
Bemrose, John [MS]
Berazaluze, Sebastián [MA]
Betty (Fleming slave; Hibernia;
      daughter of Pompey and Easter)
      [MS]
Birney, Brig. Gen. William [MS]
Bisset, Robert [MA]
* Black, Leroy [MS]
Bonham, Mr. and Mrs. Jerome [MS]
Bowles, William Augustus [DJ]
Box, James [MA]
Bravo, Christobal [MS]
Brown, John (Osauatomie) [MS]
Browne, Thomas [MA]
Bruce (Turnbull worker; New Smyrna;
      overseer) [MA]
Buchanan, James [MS]
* Bumback, Freddie [MS]
Burnett, Robert [DJ]
Butler, Maj. Pierce [DJ]

Hannah, (Old Hannah; Smith slave; worked for Anne Smith McQueen and later for Eliza McQueen Mackay) [DJ]

Harry (McQueen slave; went with Don Juan to Florida and became his trusted lifelong friend) [DJ]

Hassett, Father Thomas [MA]

Hedges, Capt. John [MA]

Henry, Maj. Guy V. [MS]

Henry (Grandmother Henry) [MS]

Herrera, Don Luciano de [MA]

Herrera, Don Sebastián de [MA]

Heyward, Thomas [MA]

Heyward, Thomas, Jr. [MA]

Hollingsworth, Timothy [DJ]

Holmes, Juan [MA]

Houstoun, Gov. John [DJ]

Howard, Carlos [DJ]

Hudson, John [MA]

Hudson, Maria Evans Fenwick Peavett [MA]

Huger, Benjamin [DJ]

Huger, Francis Kinloch (Frank) [DJ]

Huger, Mary Esther [DJ]

Huston, George [MS]

Huston, Mrs. George [MS]

Innerarity, Henrietta Panton [DJ]

Jackson, Andrew [MS]

Jarvis, Mr. [MS]

Jenckes, Hannah [MS]

Jenkins, Maj. Micah [MS]

* Jim (Little Jim; Fleming slave; son of Pompey and Easter) [MS]

Joe (Carpenter Joe; Fleming slave) [MS]

Johnson, Mr. [MS]

Johnson, William [MA]

Jones, Dr. [MS]

* July (Fleming slave; Hibernia; Betty's husband) [MS]

Katrina (Black Katrina; Don Juan McQueen's cook) [DJ]

Kirby-Smith, Gen. Edmund [MS]

Knox, William [MA, DJ]

Lafayette, Marquis de [MA, DJ]

Lafayette, Mme. [DJ]

Lang, Richard [DJ]

Las Casas, Captain General [DJ].

Laurens, Henry [MA]

L'Engle, Capt. Edward [MS]

L'Engle, John [MS]

L'Engle, Susan [MS]

Leslie, John [DJ]

* Lessie (McQueen slave; The Cottage; cook) [DJ]

Lewis, Rev. John [MA]

Lincoln, Abraham [MS]

* Liz (Fleming servant; Hibernia; cleaned guest rooms) [MS]

Llufrio, Pedro (McQueen's Minorcan houseboy) [DJ]

* Long Stem (Maria's Indian servant) [MA]

Lucy (Mama Lucy) [MA]

McClellan, Maj. Gen. George B. [MS]

McGillivray, Alexander [DJ]

McGillivray, Lachlan [DJ]

McIntosh, Col. John [DJ]

McIntosh, John Houstoun [DJ]

McIntosh, John Mohr [DJ]

Mackay, Eliza McQueen [DJ]

Mackay, Mary Anne [DJ]

Mackay, Robert [DJ]

Mackay, Robert (Robbie) [DJ]

McQueen, Alexander (Uncle Aleck) [DJ]

McQueen, Alexander [DJ]

McQueen, Ann Dalton [DJ]

McQueen, Anne Smith [DJ]

McQueen, John [DJ]

McQueen, John (Don Juan) [MA, DJ]

McQueen, John (Don Juan, Jr.) [DJ]

McQueen, Margaret Cowper [DJ]

McQueen, Sallie [DJ]

McQueen, William [DJ]

McRae, Leonard [MS]

McRae, Matilda (Tissie) Fleming [MS]

Madrid, Dr. Bernardo de la [MA]

Malloy, Lucy [MS]

Mamie (Fatio servant; Louisa Fatio's Boarding House; mother of Pootie) [MS]

Man, Spencer [MA]

Mangourit, French Colonel [DJ]

Marshall, Abraham [MA]

Marrot, Pedro [DJ]

* Mary (Indian Mary) [MS]

Mathews, Gov. George [DJ]

Mein, William [DJ]

Middleton, Arthur [MA]

Milfort, Louis [DJ]

Milton, Governor [MS]

Miró, Esteban [DJ]

Mokes, Professor [MS]

Moncrief, James [MA]

Moore, Dorothy [MA]

Moore, John [MA]

Morales, Col. Bartolomé [DJ]

Morehead, Capt. Bill [MS]
Morel, Dr. [MS]
Moultrie, James [MA]
Moultrie, Dr. John [MA]
Moultrie, Gov. William [DJ]
Mulcaster, Frederick George [MA]
Mulcaster, Jennie [MA]

Nita, Señora [MA]

* O'Hern, Mr. [MS]
Ogilvie, Maj. Francis [MA]
Oglethorpe, Gen. James [DJ]
O'Reilly, Father Miguel [DJ]
Osceola [MS]
* Owen (Big Owen; Fleming slave; Hibernia) [MS]

Pablo (Minorcan servant; worked for Maria) [MA]
Paine, King [DJ]
Palma, Antonio [MA]
Panton, William [DJ]
Peale, Raphaelle [DJ]
Peale, Rembrandt [DJ]
Peavett, Capt. Joseph [MA]
Peavett, Margaret [MA]
Pellicer, Sgt. José [DJ]
Penman, James [MA]
Pérez, Antonia de Herrera [MA]
Pérez, Diego [MA]
Pérez, Felicia [MA]
Perpal, Juan [DJ]
Perpal, Señor Antonio [DJ]
Perpal, Señora Ysabel [MA, DJ]
Pierce, Franklin [MS]
Pierce, William [MA]
Pitcher, Reuben [DJ]
* Pitts, Stoney [MS]
Plowden, William [DJ]
Polly (Fatio slave; New Switzerland; married to Scipio, a free Negro) [MS]
Pompey (William Panton's servant; knew Don Juan when both were young in South Carolina) [DJ]
* Pompey (Fleming slave; Hibernia; married to Maum Easter) [MS]
* Pootie (House servant at Fatio Inn; Mamie's daughter) [MS]
Prévost, Col. Augustine [MA]
Puente, Don Josef Elixio de la [MA]

Quesada, Gov. Juan Nepomuceno de [DJ]
Quesada, Doña Maria Josefa de [DJ]

Quesada, Roberto [DJ]

Reed, Mr. and Mrs. A. M. [MS]
* Rina (Fleming slave; Hibernia; daughter of Maum Betty and July) [MS]
Rocque, Don Mariano de la [MA, DJ]
Romero, Manuel [DJ]
Rutledge, Edward [MA]
Rutledge, Hugh [MA]

* Scipio (Fatio servant; New Switzerland; free Negro) [MS]
Scott, Gen. Winfield [MS]
Seagrove, James [DJ]
Seraphim, Father [DJ]
Seton, Charles [MS]
Seton, George [MS]
Seton, Matilda Sibbald [MS]
Seton, Capt. William [MS]
Seward, Mr. [MS]
Shaw, Col. James [MS]
Sibbald, Charles [MS]
Sibbald, Mrs. Charles [MS]
Smith, Elizabeth Williamson [DJ]
Smith, John [DJ]
Smith, Josiah [MA]
Smith, Lizzie (Mrs. Judge) [MS]
Solána, Don Manuel [MA]
Solána, Doña Maria Mestre [MA]
Stephens, Augustina (Tina) Fleming [MS]
Stephens, Clark [MS]
Stephens, Winston [MS]
Stephens family [MS]
Steward, Elder James [MS]
Stewart, General [MS]
Stowe, Harriet Beecher [MS]
Strephon (McQueen slave; The Cottage; went to Florida with Don Juan) [DJ]
Stuart, John [MA]
Sudlow, Isabel (Belle) Fleming [MS]
Summer, Mr. [MS]

Tate, John Edward (Juan Eduardo) [MA]
Telfair, Gov. Edward [DJ]
Thackeray, William Makepeace [MS]
* Thomas (Black Thomas; The Cottage; went to Florida with Don Juan) [DJ]
Thompson, Wiley [MS]
* Tiernan, Mr. [MS]
Timothy, Peter [MA]
Tonyn, Gov. Patrick [MA, DJ]

Toombs, Sen. Robert [MS]
Travers, Dr. [DJ]
Turnbull, Dr. Andrew [MA, DJ]

Wagnon, John Peter [DJ]
Wagnon, Robert [DJ]
Wallace, John [DJ]
Washington, George [DJ]
Watrin, M. [DJ]
Watson, William [MA]
Ward, Colonel [MS]
Warren, Col. John [MS]
Wayne, Gen. Anthony [DJ]
Weightman, Dr. [MS]
White, Gov. Enrique [DJ]
* White Tail [MS]
Wiggins, Job [DJ]
Willfrid (Sabre Boy; Fatio free servant;
    worked at the St. Augustine
    boarding house) [MS]
Wright, Lady Sarah Williamson Smith
    [DJ]

Ximénez, Andres [MS]

Yeats, David MA]
Ysnardy, Don Miguel [DJ]

Zamoramo, Don Gonzalo [DJ]
Zéspedes, Governor [DJ]
Zubizarreta, Señor José [DJ]

Part 3 *Savannah Quartet [SA, TS,*
    BD, SS]

Adams, John Quincy [BD]
Anderson, Capt. John [SS]
* Annie (Grange Annie; Mackay house
    servant; married to Solomon) [SA]
Arnold, Maj. Richard D. [SS]
Ash, Mr. and Mrs. John H. [SA]

Babcock, Maj. Samuel [TS]
Baines, Robert [TS]
Barnsley, Anna [BD, SS]
Barnsley, Godfrey [TS, BD]
Barnsley, Julia Henrietta Scarbrough
    [SA, TS, BD, SS]
Barnsley, Reginald [BD]
Barry, J. [BD]
Bartow, Capt. Francis S. [SS]
Battersby, William [SS]

Beauregard, Brig. Gen. Pierre [SS]
* Bentley, Fred [TS]
Benton, Thomas [BD]
Bertha (Low servant; personal maid to
    Mary Cowper Stiles Low;
    Midnight's mother) [SS]
* Biddle, Obijah (Bije) [BD]
Black, E. J. [BD]
Blake, Joe [TS]
Bolton family [SA]
Boucher, Adrian [SA]
Boudinot, Chief Elias [TS]
Bragg, Gen. Braxton [SS]
Brasch, Mr. [SA]
Breckinridge, John Cabell [SS]
Brown, John (Osauatomie) [SS]
Brown, Gov. Joseph Emerson [SS]
Brown, Dr. Lester [TS]
* Browning, Bending Willow (Ben) [SS]
* Browning, Caroline Cameron [SA, TS,
    BD, SS]
* Browning, Jonathan [TS, BD, SS]
* Browning, Mark, Sr. [SA, TS]
* Browning, Mark [SA, TS, BD, SS]
* Browning, Mary (Merry) Willow
    McDonald [TS, BD, SS]
* Browning, Melissa Cotting [SA, TS]
* Browning, Natalie (Aunt Nassie) [SA,
    TS, BD]
* Browning, Willow [SS]
Bryan, Delia Forman [SA]
Bryan, Joseph [SA]
Buchanan, James [BD, SS]
Bulloch, Dr. [BD]
Bulloch, James Stephens [SS]
Bulloch, Mittie [SS]
Bulloch, William [TS]
Burrick, Tom [SS]
Butler, Maj. Pierce [SS]
Byrom, Charles [TS]

Calhoun, John C. [SA, BD, SS]
* Cameron, Ethel [SA, TS, SS]
* Cameron, Jon [SA]
* Cameron, Jonathan [SA, TS, BD]
Campbell, Commodore Hugh G. [SA]
* Cannon, Mr. [TS]
Carter, Rev. Abiel [SA]
Cass, Gen. Lewis [BD]
Charlton, Robert M. [TS]
Charlton, Judge T. U. P. [SA]
Circoply, Captain [SS]
Claghorn, Capt. Joseph [SS]
* Clack, James [BD]
Clay, Henry [BD, SS]
* Clay, Perry [SS]

Clinch, Maj. Duncan L. [SS]
Cobb, Howell [BD]
Cockburn, Rear Adm. Sir George [SA]
* Coffey, Captain [TS]
Cohen, Fanny [SS]
Colquitt, Walter T. [BD]
Cooper, M. A. [BD]
* Cotting, Mary (Cameron indentured
     servant; mother of Melissa and
     Osmund) [SA, TS]
Couper, James Hamilton [TS, SS]
Cowper, Sir Basil [SA, SS]
Cowper, Mary Smith [SA]
Cumming, Dr. John [TS]
Cummings, John [TS]
Cummings, Elma [TS]
Cuyler, Richard [BD]

Daniell, Tom [BD, SS]
Daniell, Dr. William Coffee [BD, SS]
Davis, Captain [TS]
Davis, Jefferson [SS]
De Lyon (D'Lyon), Levi [BD, SS]
* Domer (Little Domer; Osmund Kott's
     friend) [TS]
Douglas, Stephen [SS]
Drayton, Percival [SS]
Drayton, Gen. Thomas [SS]
duBignon, Capt. Charles [SS]
Dubois, Captain [TS]
* Duffy, Mr. [BD]

* Earl (Andrew Low's driver) [SS]
Early, Gen. Jubal [SS]
Elliott, Corinne [SS]
Elliott, Sen. Daniel Stuart, Sr. [SS]
Elliott, Daniel Stuart, Jr. [BD, SS]
Elliott, Lucinda Sorrel [SS]
Elliott, Matilda Moxley [SS]
Elliott, Right Rev. Stephen [SS]
* Emphie (Mackay slave; baked
     delicious benne-seed cookies and
     biscuits) [SA, TS, BD, SS]
Esterhazy, Count [BD]
* Eunice (Sorrel maid) [SS]
Evarts, Jeremiah [TS]
* Ezra (Stiles servant; Etowah Cliffs;
     groom) [SS]

Fenn, Zechariah [TS]
Fillmore, Millard [SS]
Fletcher, Mrs. [BD]
Floyd, Brig. Gen. John B. [SA, SS]
Foreman, Col. Tom [SS]
Fraser, Frances Anne Wylly [TS]
Fremont, John Charles [BD, SS]

Gallie, Major [SS]
Geary, Gen. John [SS]
Genet, Jean [SA]
Gilmer, Captain [SS]
Girard, Stephen [SA]
Glenn, Mr. and Mrs. [SS]
Goethe, Baroness Ottilie von [BD]
Goodman, Mrs. [SS]
Goodman, Robert McAlpin [SS]
Gordon, Eleanor [SS]
Gordon, George [BD]
Gordon, Guilielma [BD]
Gordon, Nellie Kinzie [SS]
Gordon, Sarah [BD]
Gordon, William Washington [TS, BD]
Gordon, William Washington (Willie)
     [BD, SS]
Graham, Jessie Low [SS]
Grant, Ulysses S. [BD, SS]
* Gray, Mrs. [SS]
Greeley, Horace [SS]
Green, Andrew Low [SS]
Green, Charles [BD, SS]
Greene, John Holden [SA]
Guthrie, Mary Low [SS]

Habersham, Joseph, Jr. [SA]
Habersham, Robert W. [SA, BD]
Habersham, Mrs. [TS]
Hammil, Mr. [SS]
Hannah (Old Hannah; Smith slave
     belonging to Eliza McQueen
     Mackay; Hero's wife) [SA, TS, BD,
     SS]
Haralson, H. A. [BD]
Haralson, Mrs. [BD]
Hardee, William Joseph [SS]
Harris, Mayor Charles [SA]
Harrison, William Henry [BD]
Hero (Mackay slave; married to Old
     Hannah) [SA]
Hewitt, Mrs. [BD]
Hickman, Mr. [TS]
Hitchcock, Col. Ethan Allen [BD]
Hodgson, Mr. [BD]
Holder, David [BD, SS]
Holder, Elizabeth [BD]
Hood, Gen. John Bell [SS]
Hopkins, Matt [SS]
Howard, Rev. Charles [BD]
Howard, Frances [SS]
Howard, Janet [SS]
Huger, Mary Elizabeth [SS]
Hughes, Sallie [TS]
Hull, Capt. Isaac [SA]
Humphries, Charner [BD]

Humphries, Mary [*BD*]
Hunter, David [*SS*]
Hutchinson, Robert (Bob) [*SS*]

* Jackson (Cass County clerk) [*TS*]
Jackson, Andrew [*SA, BD, SS*]
Jackson, Gen. Henry [*SS*]
Jackson, Stonewall [*SS*]
Jay, William [*SA*]
Jefferson, Thomas [*SA, BD, SS*]
* Johann (Woolsey's German servant;
    Philadelphia; butler) [*SA*]
Johnston, John [*SA*]
Johnston, Gen. Joseph E. [*SS*]
Jones, Mayor [*SS*]
Jones, Albert [*TS*]
Jones, Dr. George [*SA, SS*]
Jones, Capt. Jacob [*SA*]
Julian, Mr. [*BD*]
* July (Stiles slave; Etowah Cliffs) [*BD*]

Kelly, Brigham [*SS*]
Kenan, A. H. [*BD*]
King, Mrs. Roswell, Sr. [*SS*]
Kinzie, Juliette [*SS*]
Kinzie family [*SS*]
Kitchen, Chief Engineer [*TS*]
* Knight, Leroy [*BD, SS*]
Kollock, Dr. Henry [*SA*]
* Kott, Osmund (Osmund Cotting) [*SA,
    TS, BD*]

Lafayette, George Washington [*SA*]
Lafayette, Marquis de [*SA, BD*]
Lamar, Connie [*TS*]
Lamar, Gazaway Bugg [*TS, SS*]
Lamar, J. B. [*BD*]
Lamar, Rebecca [*TS*]
Lamar, Thomas [*TS*]
* Latimer, Burke [*TS, BD, SS*]
* Latimer, Little Burke [*BD*]
* Latimer, Callie [*BD, SS*]
* Latimer, Natalie Browning [*SA, TS, BD,
    SS*]
Law, Judge William [*SS*]
Lawton, Col. Alexander [*SS*]
Lee, Custis [*BD, SS*]
Lee, Mary Custis [*TS, BD*]
Lee, Robert E. [*BD*]
* Lettie (Cameron slave; Knightsford;
    housekeeper; married to Prince;
    mother of Mina) [*SA*]
Lincoln, Abraham [*SS*]
Low, Amy [*SS*]
Low, Andrew [*SA, BD, SS*]
Low, Catherine Mackay [*SS*]

Low, Harriet [*SS*]
Low, Juliette (Julie; Daisy) Gordon [*SS*]
Low, Mary Cowper (Mary C.;
    Marysee) Stiles [*TS, BD, SS*]
Low, Sarah Cecil Hunter [*BD, SS*]
Low, William Mackay (Willy) [*SS*]
Low baby [*SS*]
Lubomirski, Prince [*BD*]
Lumpkin, Gov. J. H. [*BD*]
Lumpkin, Martha [*BD*]

* McDonald, Bending (Ben) Willow [*TS,
    BD, SS*]
* McDonald, Green Willow [*TS, SS*]
* McDonald, Tom [*TS*]
Mackay, Delia Bryan [*TS, BD, SS*]
Mackay, Eliza McQueen [*SA, TS, BD,
    SS*]
Mackay, Jack [*SA, TS, BD*]
Mackay, Kate [*SA, TS, BD, SS*]
Mackay, Mary Malbone Chilcott [*SA,
    SS*]
Mackay, Robert, Sr. [*SA, SS*]
Mackay, Robert [*SA, TS, BD, SS*]
Mackay, Robert (Robbie) [*SA*]
Mackay, *Sarah (Sallie)* [*SA, TS, BD, SS*]
Mackay, Virginia Sarah Bryan [*SA, TS,
    BD, SS*]
Mackay, William Mein [*SA, TS, BD, SS*]
Mackay, William, Jr. [*TS, SS*]
McNally, Mr. and Mrs. [*TS*]
McPherson, General [*SS*]
McQueen, John (Don Juan) [*SA, BD,
    SS*]
McQueen, John (Don Juan, Jr.) [*SA, TS*]
McQueen, Margaret Cowper [*SA, TS,
    BD*]
McRee, William [*SA*]
Madison, Dolly [*BD*]
Magill (Mackay servant; Causton's
    Bluff; worked for William Mackay)
    [*SS*]
Malbone, Edward Greene [*BD*]
Malbone, Godfrey [*SA, BD*]
* Marie (Woolsey's servant;
    Philadelphia; cook) [*SA*]
Marshall, Ann [*SS*]
Mason, Lowell [*SA*]
* Matthew (Cameron slave; Knightsford;
    driver) [*TS*]
Mein, Alexander [*SA*]
Mein, William [*SA*]
Meldrim, Ralph [*TS*]
Mercer, General [*SS*]
Mercer family [*BD*]
* Midgie (Low slave; nurse to Catherine

Low) [SS]
* Midnight (Low slave; one of Andrew Low's favorites; Bertha's son) [SS]
Millen, John [BD]
Milner, Arnold [TS, BD]
* Mina (Cameron slave; Knightsford; daughter of Lettie and Prince) [SA]
Monroe, James [SA]
Montgomery, James [TS]
Mordecai (Sheftall Sheftall's Servant; Savannah) [BD]
Mullins, Mr. and Mrs. [TS]

* Nellie (Cameron slave; Knightsford; personal maid to Caroline Cameron) [BD]
Neufville, Rev. Edward [TS]
Nicholl, Mayor John C. [TS]
Nightingale, Louisa [TS]
Nightingale, Mrs. Phineas Miller [TS]
Norris, John [SS]

Oglethorpe, Gen. James [SA]
Olmstead, Col. Charles [TS]
Olmstead, Florie [SS]
Olmstead family [SS]
* O'Toole, Maureen (Browning servant; Irish; cook) [TS, SA, BD, SS]

Parkman, Samuel [TS]
Parkman, Authexia [TS]
Parsons, James [SA]
Patterson, John [SA]
Peters, Mr. [SS]
Pinckney, Gen. Thomas [SA]
* Plemmons, Lorah (Latimer house-keeper; Cassville) [BD, SS]
* Plemmons, Luke [BD, SS]
* Plemmons, Sam [BD]
Plemmons, Sarah [BD]
Polk, James Knox [BD, SS]
Polk, Leonidas [SS]
Polk, Sarah Childress [BD]
Pony Boys [TS]
Pooler, Capt. R. W. [TS]
Porter, Capt. David [SA]
Potter, Bertha [BD]
Potter, Mr. Samuel [BD]
Priessnitz, Vincenz [BD]
* Prince (Cameron slave; Knightsford; married to Lettie) [SA, TS]
Proctor, G. V. [SA]
Pulaski, General [SA, TS]

Read, J. B. [SA]
Richardson, Richard [SA]

Ridge, Major [TS]
Robertson, Col. William [TS]
Rochester, Judge [TS]
Rogers, Capt. Moses [SA]
Roosevelt, Mr. [SS]
Roosevelt, Martha [SS]
Ross, Chief John [TS, BD]
Ross, Quatie [TS]
Rumner, Mrs. [BD]
* Running Deer, Uncle [TS, BD]

* Samson (Stiles slave; Vale Royal at Yamacraw; butler for Joseph Stiles) [TS]
Sanneman, Captain [BD]
Saunders, General [BD]
Scarbrough, Julia Bernard [SA, TS, BD]
Scarbrough, William [SA, TS, BD]
* Schultze, Gerta (Browning nurse for Natalie; Savannah-born German woman) [BD, SS]
Schwarz, J. G. [BD]
Scott, Gen. Winfield [TS, BD]
Screven, Capt. John [SS]
Scribbins, Paul [BD]
Sheftall, Benjamin [SA]
Sheftall, Mordecai [SA]
Sheftall, Dr. Moses [BD]
Sheftall, Sheftall [SA, TS, BD, SS]
Sherman, Gen. William Tecumseh [SS]
Silver, Dr. [TS]
Sims, Captain [SS]
* Sinai (Stiles slave; Etowah Cliffs; seam-stress; mother of Little Sinai) [BD, SS]
* Sinai (Little Sinai; Stiles slave; Etowah Cliffs; Sinai's daughter) [BD, SS]
Slidell, Ambassador [SS]
Sloat, Cmdr. John Drake [BD]
Smets, Mr. [TS]
Smith, Isaac [SS]
Solomon [SA, BD, SS]
Sorrel, Francis [SS]
Sorrel, Gilbert [SS]
Sorrel, Matilda [SS]
Sorrel, Gen. Moxley [SS]
Stephens, Alexander H. [BD]
Stevens, William [TS]
Stiles, Benjamin [TS, BD]
Stiles, Catherine Clay [TS]
Stiles, Eliza Anne (Lib) Mackay [SA, TS, BD, SS]
Stiles, Eliza Clifford (Cliffie) Gordon [BD, SS]
Stiles, Joseph [TS, BD, SS]
Stiles, Margaret Vernon Adams [TS]

Stiles, Margaret Wylly (Meg) Couper [SS]
Stiles, Robert Mackay (Bobby) [TS, BD, SS]
Stiles, William Henry (W.H.), Sr. [TS, BD, SS]
Stiles, William Henry, Jr. [BD, SS]
Stowe, Harriet Beecher [SS]
Stuart, Jeb [SS]
* Susan (Woolsey servant; Philadelphia; Scottish girl) [SA]
* Swift Bear [TS]

Tatnall, Commodore Josiah [SS]
Taylor, Charlotte Scarbrough [SA, TS, BD, SS]
* Taylor, Jupiter (Browning servant; free Negro houseman and driver) [SA, TS, BD, SS]
Taylor, Zachary (Old Rough-and-Ready) [BD]
Tefft, I. K. [TS]
* Terpin (Black Terpin; Savannah dock worker) [SA]
Thackeray, William Makepeace [SS]
Thompson, (Old Thompson) [SA]
Tocqueville, Alexis de [BD]
* Tom (Browning Shipping Company; clerk) [SS]
Toombs, Sen. Robert [SS]
Tread, Jeremy [BD]
Troup, Gov. George Michael [SA]
* Two Bears, Chief [TS]
Tyler, John [BD]

Tyler, Mrs. John [SS]
Tyler, Julia Gardiner [SS]

Vann, James [TS]
Vann, Chief Joseph (Rich Joe) [TS]
Villers, M. Petit de [SA]

Walker, Leroy Pope [SS]
Ward, John E. [SS]
Waring, Dr. [SA]
Warrington, Capt. Lewis [SA]
Washington, George [BD, SS]
Wayne, Adj. Gen. Henry [SS]
Wayne, Judge James Moore [SA, BD, SS]
Weld, Angelina Grimke [SA, BD]
Weld, Theodore [SA, BD]
* Wheeler, Effie [TS]
* Wheeler, Olin [TS, BD]
White, Rev. George [TS]
Williams, Lt. Robert [BD]
Williams, William Thorne [SA, TS, BD]
Wilmot, David [BD]
Wiltberger, Captain [BD]
Wise, Governor [SS]
Wool, Gen. John E. [BD]
* Woolsey, Myrtle [SA]
* Woolsey, Woodrow [SA, BD]
Worcester, Samuel [TS]
Wright, Ambrose R. [BD]
Wright, Governor (Sir James) [BD]

* Zechariah (Sorrel servant; portly butler) [SS]

Select Bibliography

This bibliography is by no means the complete record of all the works and sources consulted. Not listed are maps, photographs, pamphlets, brochures, and articles, nor the personal interviews, conversations, and correspondence from more than twenty years of interest in and study of the people and places in *Eugenia Price's South*. For the most part, books or booklets that are available on location or through libraries have been included.

Bartram, William. *Travels*. Edited by Edward Hoagland, 1988.

Bell, Malcolm, Jr. *Major Butler's Legacy: Five Generations of a Slaveholding Family*, 1987.

Bennett, Charles E. *Florida's "French" Revolution, 1793–1795*, 1981.

Blackburn, Joyce. *The Bloody Summer of 1742: A Colonial Boy's Journal*, 1984.

———. *James Edward Oglethorpe*, 1970.

Boyd, Kenneth W. *Georgia Historical Markers: Coastal Counties*, 1991.

Cate, Margaret Davis. *Hawkins-Davison Houses, Frederica: St. Simons Island, Georgia*, 1956.

Cofer, Loris D. *Queensborough: Or the Irish Town and Its Citizens*, 1977.

Coleman, Kenneth, ed. *A History of Georgia*, 1991.

Crutchfield, James A. *The Georgia Almanac and Book of Facts, 1989–1990*, 1988.

Cunyus, Lucy Josephine. *History of Bartow County, Georgia—Formerly Cass*, 1989.

Davis, Robert Scott, Jr. *A History of Montgomery County, Georgia, to 1918,* 1992.

Fleming, Francis P., ed. *Memoir of Capt. C. Seton Fleming of the Second Florida Infantry, C.S.A.,* 1881.

Fox-Genovese, Elizabeth. *Within the Plantation Household: Black and White Women of the Old South,* 1988.

Gleason, David King. *Antebellum Homes of Georgia,* 1987.

Graham, Abbie Fuller. *Old Mill Days: St. Simons Mills, Georgia, 1874–1908,* 1976.

Green, Edwin R., and Mary A. Green (illus.). *St. Simons Island: A Summary of Its History,* 1982.

Griffin, Patricia C. *Mary Evans: A Woman of Substance.* Booklet, 1977.

Hartridge, Agnes Campbell. *The Goulds of St. Clair and Black Banks, St. Simons Island, Georgia.* Privately owned manuscript.

Hartridge, Walter Charlton. *The Letters of Don Juan McQueen to His Family,* 1943.

Harvey, Karen. *St. Augustine and St. Johns County: A Pictorial History,* 1980.

Head, Joe F. *The General: The Great Locomotive Dispute,* 1990.

Huckabee, Weyman C. *Historic Glimpses of St. Simons Island, 1736–1924,* 1973.

Jolley, Clyde W., ed. *Historic Bartow County, 1828–1866,* 1981.

King, Spencer B., Jr. *Darien: The Death and Rebirth of a Southern Town,* 1981.

Lewis, Bessie, and Mildred Huie (illus.). *Patriarchal Plantations of St. Simons Island,* 1974.

——. *Hampton Plantation at Butler Point on St. Simons Island, Georgia, Plantations of Coastal Georgia.* Vol. 1, 1978.

——. *King's Retreat Plantation: Today and Yesterday, Plantations of Coastal Georgia.* Vol. 2, 1980.

McKee, Gwen, ed. *A Guide to the Georgia Coast.* Rev. ed., 1988.

Mahon, John K. *History of the Second Seminole War, 1835–1842.* Rev. ed., 1967.

Manucy, Albert. *The Houses of St. Augustine, 1565–1821,* 1992.

Marion, John Francis. *The Charleston Story: Scenes from a City's History,* 1978.

Martin, Van Jones, and Beth Lattimore Reiter. *Coastal Georgia*, 1985.

Miles, Jim. *Fields of Glory: A History and Tour Guide of the Atlanta Campaign*, 1989.

Mitchell, William Robert, Jr. *Classic Savannah: History, Homes and Gardens*, 1978.

Morrison, Mary L. *Historical Savannah: Survey of Significant Buildings in the Historic and Victorian Districts of Savannah, Georgia*, 1979.

Murphy, Mary Dean, and Mildred Nix Huie. *Kelvin Grove Plantation, 1736–1986: Hallowed Ground of the Military Road, the Battle of Bloody Marsh, the Cater-Armstrong-Postell Plantation, and St. Simons Beaches*, 1986.

Perkerson, Medora Field. *White Columns in Georgia*, 1952.

Price, Eugenia. *At Home on St. Simons*, 1981.

———. *Diary of a Novel: The Story of Writing* Margaret's Story, 1980.

———. *Inside One Author's Heart: A Deeply Personal Sharing with My Readers*, 1992.

———. *St. Simons Memoir: The Personal Story of Finding the Island and Writing the St. Simons Trilogy of Novels*, 1978.

Sherwood, Rev. Adiel. *A Gazetteer of the State of Georgia*, 1827. Reprint, 1939.

Shofner, Jerrell. *Florida Portrait: A Pictorial History of Florida*, 1990.

Sieg, Chan. *The Squares: An Introduction to Savannah*, 1984.

Steele, Richard E., Jr. *Georgia on My Mind*, 1992.

Vanstory, Burnette. *Flags of Five Nations: A Collection of Historical Sketches and Stories of the Golden Isles of Guale*, 1971.

———. *Georgia's Land of the Golden Isles*, 1956.

Waterbury, Jean Parker. *"The Oldest House": Its Site and Its Occupants, 1650 (?) to the Present*. Booklet, 1984.

———. ed. *The Oldest City: St. Augustine, Saga of Survival*, 1983.

———. *The Ximénez-Fatio House: "Long Neglected, Now Restored"*. Booklet, 1985.

Williams, Frances Leigh. *A Founding Family: The Pinckneys of South Carolina*, 1978.

Wood, Virginia Steele, ed. *Robert Durfee's Journal and Recollections . . . Saint Simons Island, Georgia (ca. 1785–1810)*, 1990.

———. *St. Simons Island, Georgia—Brunswick and Vicinity: Description and History Written by William W. Hazzard—1825*, 1974.

Index

Wright, Maj. Samuel, 22, 43
Wylly, Capt. Alexander
Campbell, 29, 37–38
Wylly, Alexander William,
38
Wylly, Caroline. *See*
Couper, Caroline Wylly.
Wylly, Frances Anne. *See*
Fraser, Frances Anne
Wylly.
Wylly, Heriot, 40
Wylly, John Armstrong,
39–41, 44, 56
Wylly, Margaret
Armstrong, 37–40

Wylly, Sarah Spalding, 39
Wylly, Susan, 38–39

X
Ximénez, Andres, 96
Ximénez-Fatio House, St.
Augustine, 95–96, 105;
95, 100

Y
Yamacraw Bluff, Savannah,
141
Youth Estate (formerly Boys
Estate), Georgia, 37

Z
Zéspedes, Gov. Vicente
Manuel de, 78